We Say
NO!

We Say NO!

The Plain Man's Guide to Pacifism

H. R. L. Sheppard

Edited by
Kerry Walters

CASCADE *Books* • Eugene, Oregon

WE SAY NO!
The Plain Man's Guide to Pacifism

Copyright © 2013 Kerry Walters. All rights reserved. Except for brief quotations in critical publications or reviews, no part of this book may be reproduced in any manner without prior written permission from the publisher. Write: Permissions, Wipf and Stock Publishers, 199 W. 8th Ave., Suite 3, Eugene, OR 97401.

Cascade Books
An Imprint of Wipf and Stock Publishers
199 W. 8th Ave., Suite 3
Eugene, OR 97401

www.wipfandstock.com

ISBN 13: 978-1-62032-922-1

Cataloguing-in-Publication data:

Sheppard, H. R. L. (Hugh Richard Lawrie), 1880–1937.

    We say NO! : the plain man's guide to pacifism / H. R. L. Sheppard; edited by Kerry Walters.

    xxxviii + 134 pp. ; 23 cm. Includes bibliographical references.

    ISBN 13: 978-1-62032-922-1

    1. Pacifism. I. Title.

JX1952 S63 2013

Manufactured in the U.S.A.

Contents

"No Comfortable Business": Dick Sheppard and Christian Pacifism
    by Kerry Walters | vii

Preface | xxxv

    I   Twenty-One Years After | 1

   II   Christ and the War-Mongers | 7

  III   Trying to Take in God | 17

  IV   Inquest on John Brown's Body | 29

    V   Romance of War | 43

  VI   The Slayer of Souls | 51

 VII   If They Raped Your Sister | 64

VIII   Here Comes the Bogey Man! | 70

  IX   The Devil's Dividends | 79

    X   The White Man's Burden | 87

  XI   Red Dawn, Black Night | 99

 XII   Who Stands for Peace? | 106

XIII   Invitation to a Circus | 116

XIV   Peace Need Not Be Dull | 123

Appendices
    A   Sheppard's "We Renounce War" Letter, 16 October 1934 | 129
    B   "The Christian Attitude to War," A Sermon Preached by Dick Sheppard at St. Mary Woolnoth, 26 February 1937 | 131

"No Comfortable Business"
Dick Sheppard and Christian Pacifism

"Jesus Christ cannot be identified with the bestial brutalities that war produces . . . [The Church] is obliged to outlaw all war and to demand from its members that they should refuse to kill their brethren."

DICK SHEPPARD[1]

*T*HE *LONDON TIMES*, APPARENTLY thinking it unseemly, refused to run it. But the *Manchester Guardian* and several provincial papers published the curious letter sent them by the Reverend Hugh Richard Lawrie Sheppard, affectionately called "Dick" by his many friends and acquaintances. Dick Sheppard was well-known throughout Britain. Pastor for over a decade at London's St. Martin-in-the-Fields Church, former Dean of Canterbury Cathedral, King's Chaplain, Companion of Honor, radio broadcaster, best-selling author, and now a canon at St. Paul's, Sheppard's opinions meant something. So his letter, even the sadly abbreviated version of it which most newspapers printed, immediately caught the public's eye.

In the letter, which appeared on 16 October 1934, Sheppard asserted that the military pacts and armaments race by which European nations pretended to pursue peace were forms of "lunacy" that would lead to war in the future as inevitably as they had in the past. His purpose in writing the letter was to test his conviction that his fellow countrymen were as convinced as he "that war of every kind or for any cause, is not only a denial of Christianity, but a crime against humanity, which is no longer to be permitted by civilized people." It was clear that up to then, "the peace

1. H. R. L. Sheppard, *The Impatience of a Parson* (Toronto: Musson, 1927) 170, 216.

movement has received its main support from women." Now, he wrote, he wanted to know if men would "throw their weight into the scales against war." He wasn't calling for the creation of a new pacifist organization. What he wanted was a headcount of all those eligible for call-up in the event of a new war who were willing to pledge themselves to the following resolution: "We renounce war and never again, directly or indirectly, will we support or sanction another." Anyone in agreement was invited to identify himself by sending Sheppard a postcard.[2] If enough people responded, Sheppard promised to put together a public rally at some future date.[3]

Sheppard's call, written at a time when the still fresh memories of the Great War's horrors threw an alarming light on the rise of fascist and Soviet militarism, struck a chord. In just two days, twenty-five hundred responses arrived in the mail, overwhelming the local post office into which they flooded. Three days after the letter appeared, even *The London Times* had to acknowledge that Sheppard's "peace appeal was sweeping the country."[4] Postcards continued to pour in over the next weeks and months. Eventually, some 50,000 men responded. Nine months later, on a sweltering Sunday in July 1935, the rally that Sheppard had promised was held in London's Albert Hall. "We didn't know what the dickens would happen," he later said. "We didn't know whether anybody would turn up or not. And then to our amazement and astonishment, young and old men, mostly young, some of them ex-service people, packed into the Hall."[5] In fact, over 7,000 men showed up to reaffirm their pledge to renounce war. There and then, despite Sheppard's reluctance to start a new pacifist society, an organization calling itself the Sheppard Peace Movement was born. Less than a year later, at Sheppard's urging, the movement renamed itself the Peace Pledge Union (PPU). Within three more years, its membership, comprised now of women as well as men, Christian and non-Christian, included some of Britain's leading lights: the poet Siegfried Sassoon, the philosopher Bertrand Russell, novelists Aldous Huxley and A. A. Milne, and prominent religious leaders such as Maude Royden, Herbert Gray, and

---

2. Because Sheppard was out of the country at the time, the postcards were actually sent to the home of his friend and fellow peace advocate, retired Brigadier General Frank P. Crozier.

3. The complete text of Sheppard's letter is reproduced in appendix A.

4. Martin Ceadel, *Pacifism in Britain, 1914–1945: The Defining of a Faith* (New York: Oxford University Press, 1980) 178.

5. Carolyn Scott, *Dick Sheppard: A Biography* (London: Hodder and Stoughton, 1977) 211.

Donald Soper. The PPU is still very much alive and active today. It is the oldest nonsectarian peace organization in Britain, and Dick Sheppard was the immediate cause of its founding.

As a sort of manifesto for those who felt called to nonviolence because of their commitment to Christ as well as for non-Christians who opposed war, Sheppard published *We Say NO! The Plain Man's Guide to Pacifism* in September 1935, just a month after the Albert Hall rally. This little book, a classic in Christian pacifist literature, presented the case for his conviction that war was an affront to the teachings and spirit of Christ, and that consequently neither the Church nor individual Christians were justified in participating in it. But *We Say NO!* was more than a theological treatise. It also offered often shrewd observations on the danger of military alliances made in the name of peace, the romanticized allure of combat, the doctrine of just war, the exportation of violence through colonialism, and the importance of media in building anti-war movements. Although firm in his belief that as a Christian he had no choice but to oppose war, Sheppard was sensitive in the book to laborers who, often just a paycheck away from poverty, worked in munitions factories, or to physicians and clergy who, by virtue of their respective callings, felt obligated to serve everyone in need, including combat soldiers. Some accused Sheppard of inconsistency, and perhaps their criticism was just. But it was an inconsistency born from compassion, not illogic. Such compassion, inspired by the example of Jesus, was what led him to pacifism in the first place, and it was the distinguishing feature of his entire adult life.

Life

Dick Sheppard was to the manor born—in a manner of speaking. His father was a minor canon in the Chapel Royals at Windsor, and it was on the castle grounds that Dick was born on 2 September 1880, in a room that had once been occupied by Anne Boleyn. He would spend a good part of his childhood at either Windsor or St. James's Palace in London.

According to family tradition, Dick's father was a descendent of an illegitimate daughter of Napoleon Bonaparte's. But even so, neither Canon Sheppard nor his wife were particularly impressed by the royalty they served. Nor, apparently, was Queen Victoria overly fond of them. "My parents," Sheppard remembered, "were not enamored of the Queen, and I think the distaste was mutual. She was a tyrant first and last, however kindly she may have been to servants and lesser people, and it is false history to write of her otherwise."[6] Sheppard's recollection of Queen Victoria may've been colored to some extent by his adult distrust of any display of hierarchical authority, including the Church of England's.

Dick Sheppard's childhood was marred by unhappiness and the beginnings of a deep-seated sense of inferiority and incompetence which he never quite shed.[7] While still a small boy, he recalled, he was tormented by sermons and pamphlets about the Day of Judgment, and for a time was awakened night after night by horrifying dreams of the apocalypse. To make matters worse, his paternal grandfather, who seems to have been something of a brute, regularly bullied him. Sheppard remembered one particularly harrowing experience with the old man. It occurred shortly after the boy had started his formal schooling. "He knew I was frightened of him," Sheppard recalled, "and he delighted in making me feel awkward and unhappy. One day while the two were seated on a park bench, Sheppard's grandfather began "asking me the meaning of *tempus fugit*, and though I knew, I was too terrified to utter the words. After a dissertation on wasting my father's slender resources [on tuition], we sailed away on a perfect hurricane of attack."[8]

The dispiriting effects of his grandfather's bullying were bad enough. But when his parents sent him away to a boarding school, twelve-year-old Dick's misery increased tenfold. He hated the place from the moment he set foot in it, not the least because he was tormented by a Latin instructor there in much the same way he had been emotionally abused by his grandfather. Years later, Sheppard still remembered one especially traumatic episode. While in Latin class, he was called upon to translate a passage from Virgil. But before he could begin, the teacher "knocked all the stuffing out of me by saying 'Let us hear what our little fool has to say.' As I stood up I was literally blinded with fear, and remained speechless, then—horror of horrors—tears

---

6. Scott, *Dick Sheppard*, 16.

7. After Sheppard's death, his colleague Maude Royden wrote: "He was apt to speak of himself as a nit-wit but when one day I protested with exasperation against this habit, he did not insist that he really was a third-class intelligence. He left that on one side and said only that he had been unhappy at school (bullied I understood) and had in consequence acquired an inferiority complex of which he could never get rid. I regretted it because it gave people who had not one tithe of his intelligence an excuse for treating him as a golden-hearted fool, and this was a fantastic misrepresentation" (Maude Royden, "Dick Sheppard: The Peacemaker," in *Dick Sheppard: An Apostle of Brotherhood* (London: Chapman & Hall, 1938) 75).

8. R. Ellis Roberts, *H. R. L. Sheppard: Life and Letters* (London: John Murray, 1942) 10.

began to trickle down my face. There was a pause, and again the voice of the master: 'I *am* sorry, Sheppard, for your Mother and Father. It must be dreadful for them to have a son like you.'"⁹ Dick became so desperate to leave the school that he doused himself with cold water each night and slept in drenched pajamas in the hope of getting sick enough to be sent home. After a year and a half, his strategy finally worked. Coming down with a bad case of pneumonia, he left the school when he was fourteen and was privately tutored throughout the rest of his teen years.

As he grew into young adulthood, the only thing about which Sheppard seemed certain was that he had no desire to follow his father into the priesthood. When the Boer War broke out, he decided to follow in the footsteps of an elder brother who had already decided on an army career, and managed to obtain a commission. But an accident in February 1900 severely injured him, putting an end to his military prospects and leaving him with a lifelong limp. After a long convalescence, he matriculated at Trinity College, Cambridge, where he was an undistinguished scholar but well-liked by his fellow students. Because it took him so long to recover from his injury, he was a bit older than the typical undergraduate.

Upon his graduation in 1904, Sheppard began working at a settlement house, Oxford House, in London's East End. (The irony of a Cambridge man at an establishment founded and funded by Oxford University wasn't lost on him.) The settlement house movement, launched in the 1880s, was a reformist effort that sought to establish centers in poor urban areas to provide services such as medical and nursery care and educational and recreational activities to local residents. Young university men (and, later, women) volunteered to live and work in the centers either during summer vacations or, like Sheppard, for a period immediately following graduation. Doing so was often considered part of a well-bred young man's educational experience, exposing him as it did, most likely for the first time in his protected middle-class life, to the overcrowding, crime, poor education, and squalor that often accompanied urban poverty.

Some settlement house volunteers found the experience too much of a shock and left after a short while. But Dick Sheppard, who went to Oxford House with vague intentions of using the experience to launch a political career, took to the work. True, he was appalled at the poverty, misery, and sometimes outright viciousness he encountered there. But as he later said, he encountered Christ in the faces of the boys with whom he primarily

---

9. Scott, *Dick Sheppard*, 21.

worked. Oxford House changed his mind about both a political career and the priesthood. In 1906, after serving a short stint as private secretary to Cosmo Lang, future Archbishop of Canterbury, Sheppard enrolled in Cuddeston College in preparation for ordination. Although he found the experience initially uncongenial, he stuck it out, and was soon as popular as he'd been at Cambridge. He was ordained a deacon in 1907 and appointed chaplain of Oxford House shortly afterwards. Two years later, he was priested and appointed head of the House.

Sheppard stayed four years at Oxford House, genuinely loving his work and the people he served. He threw himself into transforming the settlement house into a vibrant community center which offered both material and spiritual assistance to whoever asked. It was during this period that he fell into the habit of driving himself relentlessly, often working long stretches of twenty-hour days until he eventually collapsed from exhaustion. His health, already somewhat frail, would be shattered in later years by his frenetic pace. Even he recognized that his self-destructive work habits probably stemmed from the sense of inferiority instilled in him by his overbearing grandfather and his miserable school days. Throughout his entire adult life, Sheppard felt the need to overextend as a means of proving himself. It made him a dedicated and empathic pastor, but at a colossal personal cost.

The many people to whom Sheppard ministered at Oxford House came to respect and love him for his dedication and cheerful willingness to go the extra mile for them. One especially touching testimony of the high regard in which they held him came in 1936, a year before his death and a full quarter-century after he left the East End. A London bobby rang the House to ask if there was someone who worked there named H. R. L. Sheppard. A homeless man had been found dead in the streets, and the only scrap of paper on him was a note on Oxford House stationary written and signed by Sheppard. The anonymous man had carried the paper with him for twenty-five years. At the end, it was his sole possession.

Sheppard left Oxford House in 1911 after his overwork brought on a total physical collapse. For the next three years, while regaining his strength, he served as chaplain-at-large to Cosmo Lang, now Archbishop of York, and shepherded a couple of moribund West London parishes into which he infused new vitality. His superiors were so impressed with him that in July 1914, they offered him the equally moribund St. Martin-in-the-Fields parish, whose Christopher Wren-inspired church was in Central London's

Trafalgar Square. Sheppard had some doubts about accepting the assignment, and many of his friends warned him against it as well. St. Martin-in-the-Fields, they told him, was a church whose better days were long past. So far as they were concerned, the appointment was a career-killer. But Sheppard eventually accepted, believing it a great opportunity, by virtue of the church's location and history, for preaching the gospel.

Shortly afterwards, World War I, the "war to end all wars," erupted. Sheppard's installation at St. Martin's wasn't scheduled until November, so he decided to spend the intervening months as a chaplain in a military hospital in France. Unlike many of his fellow countrymen, Sheppard wasn't enthusiastic about the war, wasn't eager for active duty, and never planned to stay in France beyond the time to which he committed. But neither was he a pacifist at this point in his life.

Sheppard's two mentors, his father and Archbishop Lang, strongly disapproved of his decision, each sensing that his pattern of over-extending himself could well result in another breakdown. They were right. Once overseas, Sheppard threw himself into ministering to the maimed soldiers arriving by the thousands from the front. He was emotionally traumatized by their horrible wounds and terrific agony, and he quickly became physically exhausted from sitting round the clock with dying men. One military doctor who observed Sheppard in France later spoke of him in exasperated but admiring terms.

> He had no right to be so reckless, so stupidly careless of the elementary rules which govern fatigue and strain. He would identify himself with every dying man, and in consequence he nearly killed himself. It was wicked! Why, he would sit up all night with a case, some soldier, unconscious, kept alive only by natural strength and youth, unable to see or whisper or make any sign, except, as death came closer, to grip Sheppard's hand. Sit there, just because he had promised the dying man that he would, just because he thought it might somehow comfort the poor fellow.[10]

Predictably, Sheppard lasted only two months before he returned to England a broken man. He was nursed back to health by a young woman named Alison Carver, whom he married a year later, and was able to begin his duties at St. Martin's on schedule. But he remained haunted by his time in France for the rest of his life, and his experiences there sowed the seeds of his later pacifism.

10. Roberts, *H. R. L. Sheppard*, 84.

"No Comfortable Business"

During his twelve years as St. Martin's rector, Sheppard reinvigorated the dying parish. Only eleven people, most of them aged, bothered to show up at his installation, and average attendance at both Sunday services was barely fifteen people. The changes Sheppard inaugurated in the church—offering daily Eucharists, eliminating private pews, holding annual festivals, regularly hosting guest lecturers, turning the parish magazine into a nationally read literary and theological journal, opening the church's crypt into a shelter for soldiers on leave during the war and for the homeless afterwards, and broadcasting worship services over the BBC (Sheppard was a genuine pioneer in religious broadcasting)—angered some of the parish's longtime and more stodgy members, and a few of them deserted. But for the most part, Sheppard's tireless work, infectiously exuberant personality, deep compassion, and exciting vision awakened enthusiasm in current members and attracted new ones by the dozens. By the time he left St. Martin's in 1926—he had begun to suffer horribly from asthma, and his years of burning the candle at both ends led to yet another collapse—he had made a national name for both the church and himself. And like the homeless man who cherished a bit of paper simply because it bore Sheppard's autograph, people who came into contact with him during the St. Martin's years remembered him with affection and gratitude. One of them was a young girl who had run away to London from her home in Scotland because of a tiff with her parents. Sheppard discovered her sitting in St. Martin's crypt, encouraged her to tell him her story, walked her to the train station, bought tickets for both of them, and rode north with her to her home to make sure that her parents welcomed her. Then he caught the night train back to London. For the rector of St. Martin's, it was all in a day's work. For the girl, it meant everything in the world.

It was during those same years of tireless parish ministry that Sheppard grew increasingly dissatisfied with what he saw as the Church of England's spiritual timidity, top-heavy bureaucracy, entrenched classism, and complacent neglect of pressing social issues such as the poverty he had encountered in his years at Oxford House or the madness of war he'd witnessed in France. He was impatient with theological abstractions and the cautious conservatism of institutional religion, preferring instead to depend on the Gospels' straightforward account of Jesus' life and teachings as his moral and pastoral guide. He wanted, he told friends, to shake the Church up.[11]

11. Sheppard, *The Impatience of a Parson*, 147.

As early as 1917 he had tried to reform the Church of England by helping to found the Life and Liberty Movement, which one of his droller acquaintance's referred to as Sheppard's "gawdsakery"—*for God's sake, do something!*—movement. Partnering with future Archbishop of Canterbury William Temple, Sheppard especially wanted to "do something" about the exclusion of women from ecclesial councils, the Church's refusal to give parishioners any say in either the selection or retention of their priests, and the cronyism that bestowed the wealthiest parishes upon priests who already had substantial private means. Sheppard eventually grew disenchanted with Life and Liberty because he thought its directors, including Temple, unwilling to call for genuine reform. Despite his unhappiness, however, the movement successfully lobbied for the Enabling Act of 1919, which granted the Church of England semi-autonomy from the government. This was a large and necessary first step in the direction of the reform Sheppard wanted.

During the long and dreary months of convalescence following his resignation from St. Martin's, Sheppard began writing a book that he hoped would ignite the fire that the Life and Liberty Movement hadn't. He wasn't a novice author. He'd served as editor and contributor to the nationally acclaimed *St. Martin's Review*, and he'd already published a couple of small popular volumes, one a book of advice to fellow priests (*The Human Parson*, 1924) and the other a collection of Easter meditations (*Two Days Before*, 1924). Although both had been tamely conventional, a hint of Sheppard's growing frustration with the Church can be found in *The Human Parson*. "Our Lord would have no quarrel," he wrote, "with anyone who struck out a new line or was searching for a new truth. There is no one who rejoices more in the adventurer."[12] The book he began composing while recovering from his breakdown was certainly adventurous. Its title, *The Impatience of a Parson*, expressed both the author's mindset and the urgency of his message.

Impatience was the fruit of Sheppard's growing distaste for what he saw as the Church of England's loss of touch with what really mattered in the Christian life. Clergy, he worried, distanced themselves from their parishioners; theologians made crooked the straightforward teachings of Christ; and bishops wasted their time and energy on insignificant ecclesial matters while neglecting the church's responsibility to preach peace with justice. All of this, Sheppard believed, was a betrayal of Christ. "I could more easily see Our Lord sweeping the streets of London," he declared, "than issuing edicts

12. H. R. L. Sheppard, *The Human Parson* (London: John Murray, 1935) 85.

from its cathedral." Jesus was a "constructive revolutionary and a most uncompromising destroyer of all that was decadent and hurtful to the soul of man" who had no respect for institutionalized religion.[13] Sheppard longed to reintroduce the Galilean's constructive revolution. And the best way to do that was to return to "a fresh edition of Christianity, with the teaching of the Sermon on the Mount as its creed."[14]

Sheppard wasn't sure how his book would be received by the public, but he had little doubt that his harsh criticism of the Church as "a caricature of what Christ intended" would destroy his chances of ever getting another parish. When *The Impatience of a Parson* appeared in October 1927, it became an instant bestseller. By the time of his death almost exactly ten years later, the book had sold over 100,000 copies, vindicating Sheppard's intuition that there were tens of thousands of people who shared his impatience with a business-as-usual Church. Predictably, there were members of the clergy, including some who wore purple cassocks, who intensely disliked the book. The Bishop of Gloucester even publicly called Sheppard a fool.[15] But to his surprise, Sheppard wasn't persecuted or even formally rebuked by his superiors. For the most part, the Church of England hierarchy either publicly ignored the book or referred to it in patronizing tones as the latest bee in Dick Sheppard's bonnet. This indifference both reaffirmed his worries about the Church's inertia and hurt him deeply. Better to be hotly condemned than frozen by cold indifference.

Sheppard remained an invalid for over a year after *Impatience* was published. The asthma that had forced his resignation from St. Martin's was merciless, and there were stretches of entire weeks when he could barely rise from his sickbed. But he gradually began to mend at the beginning of 1929, and soon found himself longing for another position in the Church, both because he felt the need to be active again and because he was worried about finances. Even though *Impatience* and the occasional essays he wrote for newspapers brought in some income, it wasn't quite enough to support his wife and daughter. He even thought of leaving the Church to take up some sort of secular occupation. But in May 1929 he was astounded by the offer of the Deanship of Canterbury Cathedral. The Church had called him back in

---

13. Sheppard, *The Impatience of a Parson*, 156, 139.

14. Laurence Housman (ed.), *What Can We Believe? Letters Exchanged Between Dick Sheppard and L. H.* (London: The Religious Book Club, 1939) 85.

15. Ibid., 129.

"No Comfortable Business"

from the cold, most likely at the urging of his old mentor Cosmo Lang, who had been installed as Archbishop of Canterbury only six months earlier.

Sheppard loved his time at Canterbury, and both cathedral staff and parishioners obviously loved him. He brought an unquenchable freshness to his new post that enlivened everyone who came into contact with him. But in less than a year Sheppard's old pattern of overwork broke his fragile health once more. The cathedral staff refused even to discuss the possibility of his resignation, sending him instead to the south of France to recuperate. But the climate there only worsened his breathing difficulties, and he returned to England more ill than when he left. Utterly unable to continue with his duties as Dean, and unwilling to be kept on permanent sick leave, he insisted on resigning in February 1931. To the end of his days he regretted having to leave Canterbury. When he died nearly seven years later, he was buried there, at his own request.

Ever since his wartime experiences in France, Sheppard had been moving toward pacifism. While still at St. Martin's, he had lent his pulpit to several of the nation's leading pacifist speakers, and in 1925 had written a much-discussed letter to *The London Times* protesting a ball planned for the evening of Remembrance Day, asserting that such a frivolity on a day honoring the dead of the Great War was both irreligious and indecent. By 1927, he was fully committed to Christian nonviolence and declared his allegiance in *The Impatience of a Parson* when he wrote that the Anglican Communion (and, by implication, all Christian communions) should affirm that the "brotherhood of all men, irrespective of their class or nationality or race" cannot "be reconciled with any competitive ideal of human life which necessitates that the weak must go to the wall for the benefit of the strong or that requires men to slay their brother men." Consequently, he concluded, the Church "is obliged to outlaw all war and to demand from its members that they should refuse to kill their brethren."[16]

After he left Canterbury, Sheppard's fidelity to a pacifism based on the teachings of Jesus became his abiding concern. He spoke in 1931 in Albert Hall at a No More War rally (his asthma was so bad that he collapsed at the end of his speech and was bedridden for weeks afterwards). His first major public campaign against war was launched in February 1932 in collaboration with Maude Royden, author and chief pastor of the Guildhouse, an independent London church, and Herbert Gray, Presbyterian minister, former army chaplain, and member of the pacifist Fellowship of Reconciliation. Together,

---

16. Sheppard, *The Impatience of a Parson*, 216.

xvii

they planned to enlist a "Peace Army" of Christian pacifists who would travel to embattled areas and physically place themselves between opposing forces. In the eyes of many, the Peace Army was a quixotic gesture. But others applauded it as an admirable effort to do something practical to actually prevent war instead of merely condemning it.

The idea for a Peace Army originated with Royden, who was horrified at the October 1931 Japanese invasion of Manchuria. In a sermon at the Guildhouse a month later, she told her congregation that she longed "to enroll people who would be ready to put their bodies unarmed between the contending forces."[17] By February, when reports of the League of Nation's inability to prevent Japanese atrocities in Manchuria were flooding the press, Royden met with Sheppard and Gray to brainstorm about an alternative strategy, and the two men embraced her Peace Army proposal. On 25 February, a letter jointly signed by them appeared in London newspapers that called for volunteers who would travel to Shanghai, under Sheppard's leadership, to serve as human barriers between the Japanese and Chinese armies.

Although nearly 1,000 people volunteered for the Peace Army, and even though Sheppard visited Lloyd George, former prime minister of England, to enlist his support for the project, neither Sheppard nor his peace soldiers ever made it to Asia. The League of Nations refused to transport them, and the British government actively dissuaded them from embarking on the enterprise. To top things off, Sheppard once again fell ill, so desperately that this time his doctors genuinely despaired of his life. Even before this latest breakdown, his health would've never allowed him to lead the Peace Army into action, and it was foolish of him to imagine otherwise. But there's no doubt that Sheppard was perfectly earnest in his desire to do so, and that he most likely would've dragged himself to the ship had he and his fellow volunteers managed to find transportation.[18]

Although Sheppard's health continued to plague him, he began speaking as often as he could in defense of pacifism, both from the speaker's stump and in BBC radio broadcasts. In 1933 he started writing a weekly column for the *Sunday Express* that brought in a steady income and increased his popularity in England. Toward the end of his life, these newspaper pieces

17. Ceadel, *Pacifism in Britain, 1914-1945*, 94.
18. Sheppard's dream of a Peace Army was revived in 1984 by American theologian Ron Sider's call for a nonviolent peacekeeping force that would travel to conflict zones in an effort to prevent violence. Inspired by Sider's remarks, the Mennonite and Brethren in Christ Churches formed Christian Peacemaker Teams. The first mission of CPT was to Iraq in 1990, shortly before the Gulf War.

"No Comfortable Business"

were published in two book-length collections, with a third, edited by his daughter, appearing posthumously. They deal with topics ranging from virtues such as compassion to advice on using leisure time fruitfully. Some of them are banal and utterly forgettable, but others are sterling examples of sage counsel given in language stripped of theological obfuscation. One of them, entitled "Simplify Christianity!," perfectly expressed Sheppard's conviction that the Faith should be presented in a manner that illuminates rather than overcomplicates its core. "Would not this simplification of Christianity be according to the mind of Christ, Who, in His earthly pilgrimage, strove passionately and persistently to deliver the hungry crowd from the indigestible subtleties of many of their professional teachers?"[19] Given his high regard for plain speech (a quality, by the way, shared by his younger contemporary C. S. Lewis) it's not surprising that the subtitle of Sheppard's *We Say NO!* is *The Plain Man's Guide to Pacifism*.

In a slender book he published in 1935 entitled *If I Were a Dictator*—the book was in a series with the same title; each volume was written by a leading scientist or theologian of the day—Sheppard pointed out that simplifying Christ's message didn't mean watering it down. On the contrary, returning to the heart of the Gospel meant recapturing and living the constructively revolutionary spirit of Jesus.

> Christianity is a terrific explosion, lovely, dynamic; it is Godlikeness, and its primary message is as a bullet that explodes in the soul of man. That is no comfortable business. Jesus Christ was not merely wonderfully kind and friendly to this world's failures. He was that and vastly more; a great deal of His teaching was spoken in the teeth of a mob howling for His life. It is not the Church's function to be content when it has taught men to be hearty and friendly and sociable.[20]

Sheppard's health took an upward swing in 1933 after he started using a German-made "breathing apparatus" that greatly reduced the severity and frequency of his asthma attacks. Feeling steadier on his feet, he once again sought a church appointment. He was persuaded that his chief ministry was awakening Christians to Jesus' pacifist message, and he had no intention of giving it up. But he needed to earn a living, and appealed to Archbishop Lang, whose response was affectionate but frank. "Now that happily you are so well again, you become a very real and lovable

---

19. H. R. L. Sheppard, *Some of My Religion* (New York: Harper & Brothers, 1936) 45.
20. H. R. L. Sheppard, *If I Were Dictator* (London: Methuen, 1935) 44-45.

xix

"No Comfortable Business"

problem," Lang told him. "It is partly your fault and partly your merit that it is not easy to place you." But Lang *did* know of one open spot: a Canonry at London's St. Paul's Cathedral. Sheppard was reluctant to accept the appointment. As just one canon among several under the supervision of the cathedral dean, he feared being muzzled. But Lang reassured him that "it is a job which you could make your show. You would have full liberty of prophesying, though I know you would prophesy, I hope, not only destructively but constructively."[21] Although he still had serious misgivings, Sheppard accepted the appointment in late September 1934 and assumed his duties in November. He remained a canon at St. Paul's for the rest of his life, but was never quite happy there. Although given the widest of latitudes by Walter Matthews, the Dean of St. Paul's, Sheppard more than once thought about resigning.

What kept Sheppard sane was his peace work. Two weeks after his appointment to St. Paul's, his letter calling for men to renounce war appeared in the newspapers. Eight months later the organization that would soon become the Peace Pledge Union was formed at the great rally in Albert Hall, and Sheppard commenced a grueling speaking schedule on its behalf across England that continued right up to his death.[22] He traveled all over England, and in the summer of 1937 even sailed to New York to raise money for the PPU, an adventure that both exhausted and exasperated him because, as things turned out, he was never paid by the sponsors of the trip.

The final year of Sheppard's life was plagued by misfortune. In addition to the New York fiasco, his wife Alison left him for another man. She had stuck by him loyally for over twenty years, but his chronic ill health had finally worn her down. Although she eventually asked Sheppard to take her back, he died before a reconciliation with her could occur. Moreover, his health broke once more under the strain of his work (and, probably, grief) and in his final months his old enemy asthma, this time aggravated by an increasingly weak heart, returned with a vengeance.

But the sorrow of his final months was eased by two events. In the summer of 1937, sick though he was, he organized a PPU summer camp in Swanwick, Hampshire. Attended by some 500 people, the weeklong event was a great success, combining playfulness with educational seminars. It

---

21. Roberts, *H. R. L. Sheppard*, 245.

22. A sample of one of the many sermons on peace from this period, this one delivered just a few months before his death, is reproduced in appendix B.

gave Sheppard the opportunity—his final one, as it turned out—to be with those closest to him in the campaign to renounce war.

The second event that gladdened him in his final days was his election as honorary rector of Glasgow University. His main challenger for the position was Winston Churchill, one of the nation's most vociferous hawks. Sheppard beat him by a large majority and rejoiced that his election was an affirmative vote for the pacifism he defended and Churchill deplored. "This definitely puts Pacifism on the map," he said when he received word of his election. "It's overwhelming news. I'm almost weeping with happiness."[23]

The death that Sheppard had so often eluded came for him less than two weeks later during the night of 31 October 1937, as he sat at his study desk writing letters, among which was a birthday greeting to Cosmo Lang. His body was discovered the following morning.

The nation was shocked and saddened by the news of his death. On All Souls' Day, 2 November, his body was taken to his old parish of St. Martin-in-the-Fields, where it lay in state for two days. Thousands of people arrived to file past his coffin and pay their final respects. On 4 December his funeral procession to St. Paul's Cathedral was joined by hundreds more, even though the route had not been advertised so as not to tangle city traffic. Dean Walter Matthews, who delivered the eulogy, accurately remarked that out of devotion to Jesus's revolutionary message of nonviolence, Sheppard "was willing to become a fool for Christ's sake" by bucking both religious and secular convention.[24] His friend, the English author Rose Macaulay, spoke for everyone who mourned his passing. "When Dick Sheppard died," she said, "the world's temperature seemed to drop."[25]

We Say NO!

The success of *We Say NO!* immensely gratified Sheppard. Its reception was primed, of course, by his October 1934 open letter calling for a pledge against war service and the July 1935 Albert Hall rally where several thousand signers of the pledge gathered. Moreover, the book had gained notoriety even before it appeared as a bound volume in September 1935 through being serialized in the liberal weekly *Reynold's News*. When *We Say NO!* appeared in bookstores, its dust jacket immediately caught the

23. *Dick Sheppard, by His Friends* (London: Hodder & Soughton, 1938) 11.
24. Ibid., 166.
25. Scott, *Dick Sheppard*, 14.

eyes of browsers. In starkly contrasting shades of black and orange, it depicted a bird's-eye view of a thorn-crowned Christ hanging from the Cross, surrounded by a forest of deadly looking bayonets, one of them brutally thrust into his side. Copies of the book were snatched up as quickly as they could be printed. Sheppard, who dedicated the book to several of his closest collaborators, including Maude Royden and Herbert Gray, announced his intention to donate all royalties to the peace movement he'd started.

Even readers who weren't pacifists admired the book. One of them wrote to Sheppard to praise it as "the best you have done—I think you have put your case most forcibly and also finely. Almost thou persuadest me!" Others, such as Cosmo Lang and William Temple, thought the book a bit slapdash, but nonetheless admired its spirit while disagreeing with its conclusions. On the other hand, R. Ellis Roberts, Sheppard's friend and future biographer, thought the book's defense of pacifism "unsatisfactory" in both its logic and its practical implications.[26] Needless to say, Roberts wasn't the only one who disliked the book. Many of Sheppard's fellow countrymen, especially those who were pillars of church and state, found his blanket condemnation of war both religiously offensive and outrageously unpatriotic.

But Sheppard knew from the start that his message would likely be rejected by the wealthy and powerful, and that it would be heard best by young people who, raised on stories of the First World War's horrors, watched with growing alarm as Europe raced toward another conflict. Both the opening and closing of his book clearly indicated the audience Sheppard most wanted to reach. In chapter I, he recalled ministering to a dying soldier in the "war to end all wars" who "died thanking God" that his sacrifice meant his son "would never have to go through the hell of war." In sharing this memory from 1914, Sheppard chillingly noted that the dead soldier's son and the sons of all the other warriors of the Great War "are of military age today." It was to them, consequently, that he addressed his plea for peace, first because their fathers' generation had failed to end all wars, second because they were the ones who would be sacrificed if war came again. "Shall we choose Mars and the suicide of civilization, or Christ and its fulfillment?" Sheppard asked at the end of his book. "It is Youth that must decide." His aim in *We Say NO!* was to help youth make the right decision.

Sheppard made no apologies for the fundamental argument that grounded his opposition to war: war is murder on a grand scale and murder

---

26. Roberts, *H. R. L. Sheppard*, 275, 334.

is never justifiable, first because God commands "Thou shalt not kill!" and second because Christ's life and teachings demand nonviolence of his followers. Whenever war erupts, it's the consequence of Christians not having the courage of their convictions or, worse, of twisting Scripture to suit their own purposes. It won't do for Christians to point the finger at the bellicosity of tyrants as the cause of war. "It is *our* fault," the fault of Christian men and women, "because we have been unwilling to accept the practical implications of our Christianity" (chapter I). Several of Sheppard's critics objected that not all killing was murder and that consequently the Decalogue's injunction against killing need not apply to a morally justifiable war. But for Sheppard, no war could be considered justifiable for the simple reason that violence of any sort, but especially warfare, is contrary to Christ's example. As he wrote eight years before *We Say NO!* was published, "Jesus Christ cannot be identified with the bestial brutalities that war produces."[27]

Others accused Sheppard of tunnel vision because he focused exclusively on wartime killing and ignored other forms of life-taking violence such as capital punishment. If it's absolutely wrong to kill, they said, then surely capital punishment is as wicked as combat, and Sheppard was either inconsistent or insensitive to not condemn it as well. The point they missed was that Sheppard's silence on capital punishment didn't at all mean he condoned it, but only that he'd chosen to focus his attention on war. A single individual, after all, can do only so much, particularly if his energy is sapped by chronic illness, and a single book can stretch only so far.

Although Sheppard's bottom-line objection to war was his fidelity to Christ, his book's strength (in the eyes of some; it was a weakness in the eyes of others) lay in his refusal to rest his case exclusively on theological arguments. Instead, he interwove his faith-based objections to war with often trenchant practical and moral ones. Just as he wanted the Peace Pledge Union to be nonsectarian in order to attract as large a following as possible, so he wanted *We Say NO!*'s defense of pacifism to be broad enough to appeal to non-believers while at the same time affirming his own Christian commitment.

Like many pacifists before and after him, Sheppard was convinced that violence in general and war in particular were for the most part bred by fear of what he called "bogey men" (chapter VIII). These bogey men took many forms—foreign nations, people of different ethnicities or religions, the stranger in the neighborhood, the person with an unconventional

---

27. Sheppard, *The Impatience of a Parson*, 170.

lifestyle or beliefs—but they all were seen as posing a threat that needed to be met with force. Because fear and the hatred it defensively generates are infectious, it doesn't take long to whip a nation or group of people up into war frenzy. That's why the intricate network of military alliances ratified in Europe prior to World War I, as well as the out-of-control arms race entered into by the major powers, actually encouraged rather than discouraged war once a provocation occurred. "Peace precariously poised upon the points of bayonets," insisted Sheppard, was no peace at all (preface). In the 1930s, he saw a replay of the same mad rush to military alliance and armaments build-up that had led to war in 1914, the same toxic assumption on the part of governments and ordinary citizens that war was sometimes a necessary, and hence acceptable, evil (chapter I). It made no difference to Sheppard whether the military alliances that claimed to guarantee peace were negotiated by self-interested individual sovereign states or by idealistic collective bodies such as the League of Nations. "I am opposed to any peace system that is founded upon force," he wrote, because such a foundation automatically admits the possibility—and, so far as Sheppard was concerned, the inevitability—of war (chapter III).

In order to counter this conventional assumption, Sheppard went to great pains in *We Say NO!* to debunk the doctrine of just warfare (although, curiously, he doesn't actually mention it by name). This position, endorsed in one version or another by many Christians and secularists alike since formulated by Augustine in the fourth century, holds that war, when entered into under certain conditions and fought under certain constraints, can be morally acceptable. Sheppard examined several wars that typically have been accounted just ones—the American Civil War, for example, or the Greco-Persian Wars of the fifth century BCE—and concluded, first, that they inflicted more havoc than they redressed, and second, that their aims could have been better accomplished by peaceful means. Wars that are justified by either Christian patriots or humanitarians on the grounds that they are doing God's work or rescuing suffering humanity are even more susceptible than other kinds of wars to atrocities, precisely because idealistic violence always allows itself wide moral latitude (chapters II–IV). Even the best intentions in the world, such as the desire to expand civilization (chapter X) or to end repression and economic injustice, morph into brutality when the means used to achieve them is violent. It is a "fatal error" to presume that "although war generally is wrong, one particular kind of war is right" (chapter XI).

"No Comfortable Business"

Despite this, many people believe that war is a crucible which brings out the best in human beings. They maintain that it cultivates virtues such as courage, patience, endurance, and self-sacrifice. This valorization of war tends to encourage what Sheppard took to be a perversely romantic view of martial glory that sentimentalizes heroic "defeat, frustration, [and] death." Sagas such as the *Song of Roland* praise the nobility of dying in battle for one's nation, and men who fall on the battlefield are held up as paragons of courage. But Sheppard saw nothing ennobling about warfare. On the contrary, he maintained that combat is a "slayer of souls," and some of his book's more poignant sections report firsthand accounts of the ways in which military training and battle brutalize soldiers and noncombatant civilians alike. Despite high-blown rhetoric about the nobility of war, combat inevitably corrupts those who participate directly in it or who profit from it back on the home front. Sheppard found pious injunctions to World War I recruits to preserve their sexual purity hypocritical, given the inevitability that any innocence they brought with them to war would be quickly and savagely destroyed (chapter VI). But such, he believed, is the predictable blind spot of those who think that war is somehow ennobling. They strain at gnats, but swallow camels.

Although some people who champion specific wars do so out of misguided idealism, there are always those who covertly encourage it out of the hope of great personal gain. Sheppard singled out armaments manufacturers in particular as members of this reprehensible class. They pocket the "devil's dividends," all the while insisting that their hands are clean because they don't actually pull the triggers of the guns they make or toss the grenades that they sell to the world's armies. But Sheppard was impatient with this sort of rationalization. "Just as I say that it is inconsistent with the spirit of Christianity to bear arms, so I say that it is inconsistent with the spirit of Christianity to manufacture arms. I have no sympathy with the man who says, 'My religion will not allow me to serve in the Forces, but I am willing to do munitions work'" (chapter IX). He wholeheartedly agreed with his friend George Bernard Shaw, who wrote in the anti-war play *Major Barbara* that the "true faith" of an arms merchant is the unashamedly self-interested promotion of killing.

But Sheppard's exposure over the years to poverty, beginning with his early settlement house work in the East End and continuing throughout his subsequent years of public ministry, prompted a clear distinction on his part between the munitions manufacturer who cynically sold weapons of death for huge profits and the assembly line worker in the munitions factory simply trying to feed his family. Sheppard didn't deny that arms factory workers drew devil's wages just as the factory owner and his stockholders profited from devil's dividends. But he also believed there was a significant difference between them. Unlike the munitions manufacturer, the worker had everything to lose if he forsook his job because of moral or religious qualms. He wasn't in it for obscene profit margins, but simply for a survivable wage.

> The armament worker who is asked . . . to give up his job [makes] an immediate sacrifice. And it has no value whatever as a testimony, as a confession of faith.[28] Nobody will bother about his reasons for stopping work except the court of referees which disallows his claim for unemployment benefit, and the wife who finds herself with no money to pay the rent or buy food for the children. His place will be filled at once, and within a week or a day his former workmates will have forgotten him (chapter IX).

Sheppard went on to insist that his purpose wasn't to "deter a true Christian from doing what he believes to be his duty." But he felt he had no right to judge someone in such a position if he chose to remain with his job. There are competing interests at play here that have nothing to do with the cold-blooded profit motive that animates a munitions manufacturer. Instead of morally condemning a blue collar worker who, struggling to support his family, hires on with a munitions firm, we should ask ourselves why we aren't doing something about the system that gives rise to these tragic possibilities in the first place. "If it is a sin to choose the easier way [of keeping the job], we must share the responsibility of that sin, for it is we who have tempted our brothers, who have driven them into evil under the harsh compulsion of hunger" (chapter IX).

Had Sheppard been a self-righteous ideologue,[29] he would've refused to distinguish between arms merchants and munitions factory workers.

---

28. I think Sheppard overstates his case here. Individual protests against violence and injustice have often been symbolic catalysts for widespread reform. One thinks, for example, of Ruby Sales and the Civil Rights Movement, or Karen Silkwood and public awareness of the dangers of nuclear energy.

29. As he put it in a letter to his friend Laurence Housman, Sheppard worried about the "rabid orgy of self-righteousness" that both nations and individuals too often indulged in. "I think it has always been the main cause of the world's suffering and wrong—people doing horrible unChristlike things because they are sure that they are *right!* It's *then* that the evil is so doubly hard to cure" (Housman, *What Can We Believe?*, 241).

"No Comfortable Business"

But first and foremost he was a pastor who, although passionately engaged in trying to end warfare, was also concerned not to sacrifice persons for principles. Given the messy realities of the world, sometimes principle had to bend just a bit in order to accommodate compassion. The trick was in knowing how to distinguish bend from break so as to remain faithful to the principle while taking into consideration the concrete needs of actual persons. Some of Sheppard's critics, both those who shared his pacifism and those who opposed it, accused him of vacillation and even hypocrisy. But a more generous—and, I think, more accurate—reading of his position is that he saw the necessity of sometimes having to hold two competing interests in tension rather than rushing to eliminate one or the other. This both/and approach is certainly more difficult than an either/or one, because it demands an acknowledgement of ambiguity when it comes to navigating moral waters. But it's often the more compassionate one as well.

Another example of Sheppard's appreciation of moral ambiguity was his conflicted response to the 1935 Italian invasion of Abyssinia. Part of Mussolini's dream of a new Roman Empire included seizing the small east African nation of Abyssinia (Ethiopia). Beginning in 1934, a series of threats, skirmishes, and temporary treaties clearly demonstrated to the world that Abyssinia was in danger of an unprovoked Italian invasion. As the world watched with dismay Italy's escalating aggression, the League of Nations tried on several occasions to arbitrate, failing each time. In the absence of successful peace negotiations, many observers around the world believed that military intervention was the only way to ease Abyssinia's suffering, and even pacifists such as Sheppard questioned the appropriateness of nonviolence in situations such as this one. As he wrote in July 1935, "Abyssinia and Italy simply beats me. I don't know what we Pacifists ought to be at."[30] In admitting his own perplexity, Sheppard once again refused to smooth over the inevitable uncertainty of moral decision-making. He genuinely believed that as a Christian he couldn't condone violence. He also acknowledged that sitting on one's hands in the face of violence was unacceptable. But what exactly to do, especially when innocent people were suffering at the hands of aggressors, was sometimes baffling enough to keep any person of good will awake at nights.

Sheppard's reflections on the responsibilities of physicians and clergy in wartime is a third example of his recognition that sometimes principle sat uneasily with the moral obligation to help persons in immediate need.

30. Housman, *What Can We Believe?*, 240.

"No Comfortable Business"

Would signing his peace pledge mean that healers of body and soul should refuse any and all cooperation with the military? In a simple world, the answer would obviously be "yes." But given the complex nature of the real one, a more nuanced response was called for.

Physicians, by virtue of their Hippocratic Oath, pledge to come to the aid of those in medical need, and wounded soldiers obviously and often horrendously fall into that category. So on the one hand, it would seem that physicians are morally obliged to serve as military surgeons. But on the other hand, because patching up wounded soldiers inevitably means that many of them will be returned to the fighting, military surgeons have a personal hand in sending young men to possible battlefield death. This seems incompatible with their Hippocratic Oath to "do no harm," and is also an obvious violation of conscience for a pacifist physician. What's the right thing to do?

Sheppard admitted there's no easy solution to the dilemma of inhumanely sending men back to battle or inhumanely denying them medical aid. Nor did he want to renounce his pacifist opposition to participating in war. But in this case, where the need is urgent and personal, compassion deserved priority. "Personally," wrote Sheppard, "I would not like to feel that any man had lost his life because, out of a tender regard for the scruples of my own conscience, I had shut my ears to the call of human need" (chapter XII). For similar reasons, clergy cannot in good conscience refuse "to take religion to those who may need it most, to those who are in the Valley of the Shadow of Death" (chapter XII). One possibility (although Sheppard acknowledged it's not a likelihood) would be for pacifist clergy to serve as civilian missioners who would not be answerable to military authorities. But barring that, even clergy who morally condemn all war as contrary to the Lord they serve should not hesitate to minister to the needs of soldiers, provided they do so out of loving compassion and not with any intent to even implicitly condone war.

In the final two chapters of *We Say NO!*, Sheppard moved to suggestions about how to go about creating a culture of peace. He knew all too well that merely speaking out against war and war preparations wasn't sufficient. A positive alternative was called for, one that whittled away at the fear and self-righteousness that motivated violence, recommended a kind of heroism not found on the battlefield, and provided for a nondestructive outlet for all the human energy and emotion typically churned up by war.

"No Comfortable Business"

To do something about the fear and suspicion that breed war, Sheppard astutely recommended making use of all available media to break down cultural barriers between nations and encourage a spirit of international dialogue and cooperation. As a genuine pioneer in the use of radio to preach the Gospel (at one time the BBC considered naming him head of its religious broadcasting division), Sheppard appreciated the power of the media—in his day, radio, the press, and cinema—to reach extraordinarily huge audiences, and he believed that pacifists should make full use of it. "Wireless could be used by a Peace Government . . . to make known its aims to the world . . . The German would be able to hear them in German, and the Frenchman in French. And, step by step, as the great adventure proceeded, the world would be informed by wireless of the progress made" (chapter XIV).

Sheppard also proposed enlisting celebrities of the day to partner in a coordinated worldwide crusade for peace—"the greatest Crusade of all"—in what he called a traveling "Peace Circus." Respected intellectuals, activists, and artists such as Bertrand Russell, Albert Einstein, Gandhi, Charlie Chaplin, and George Bernard Shaw would raise their collective voices for peace in city and countryside, and speak with such authority that they would create an anti-war groundswell that politicians couldn't ignore. The more world leaders in the sciences, the arts, and religion jumped on board, the more powerful the influence of the Peace Circus would prove. Soon, peace would be more fashionable than war (chapter XIII).

One of the points that both the media campaign and the touring celebrity peace entourage would emphasize was that the meaning of "heroism" needed to be rethought. Typically reserved for battlefield valor, the word, Sheppard regretted, had become "a monopoly of the warrior." But, he continued,

> I have known it in humble homes, where adversity has tried the souls of men and women and found them pure gold. The widowed mother, battling to give her children food and clothing and shelter and opportunity, does not see herself as a heroine, but she needs, and displays, a courage greater than the soldier's. The man who, assailed by sickness and unemployment, a prey to the unmerited disaster, yet goes bravely on and tries to build up a career from the ruins of the old, would scoff if you called him a hero. But that is what he is (chapter XIV).

"No Comfortable Business"

Finally, just as military pageants and mock battles thrilled audiences, so peace-minded governments and societies could offer equally stimulating nonviolent opportunities for emotional release. The problem, maintained Sheppard, is that we've been taught to believe that life without the challenge of proving oneself in armed conflict is dull. But this is a falsehood. "We do not take danger or excitement out of life when we turn our backs on war" once we learn to appreciate that "ordinary, everyday life" is immensely exhilarating. There will always be dangerous adversaries to be reckoned with in the form of natural disasters, disease, and poverty. There will always be opportunities for adventure, "mountains to climb, seas and skies to navigate, unknown lands to explore, secrets of knowledge and healing to unveil." Life is "immeasurably fuller" than romanticizers of war are willing to acknowledge. The task of pacifists is to awaken people to that great truth, and to help them realize that war isn't needed to quicken pulses and infuse life with adventure (chapter XIV).

Legacy

Dick Sheppard's *We Say NO!* sheds light on the British pacifist movement between the two world wars. But it's much more than an historical document. Although many of Sheppard's specific references to events and personalities are now dated, the underlying argument for pacifism he intended them to illustrate remains pertinent today to anyone concerned about war, and especially to Christian pacifists.[31]

To a world that has witnessed the mass proliferation of both nuclear and conventional weapons of mass destruction, not to mention the huge industry that supplies them and fattens on the "devil's dividends," Sheppard's warning against the arms race and his condemnation of munitions

---

31. Chapters X and XI, respectively on colonialism and communism and fascism, will strike the contemporary reader as particularly dated. But even in them, the underlying claims made by Sheppard remain insightful. In chapter X, Sheppard argues that European culture should be wary of claiming superiority over developing nations, because one of its major exports to them is the modern arsenal of weapons which the developed world has created. In this same chapter, he also makes the case for police rather than military force in quelling disturbances, and for the use of nonlethal weaponry. In his condemnation of fascism and Soviet-style communism in chapter XI, Sheppard makes some trenchant observations about the reasons for the authoritarian state's repression of religion. He also points out, quite correctly, that in many ways both fascism and communism, despite their authoritarian tendencies, were protests against social and economic injustices ignored by more democratic societies.

"No Comfortable Business"

manufacturers are both prescient and worth heeding. His claim that war brutalizes both combatants and noncombatants has been attested to time and again in recent years as our understanding of post-traumatic stress disorder has grown. So have his cautionary words about a nationalistic self-righteousness that conducts crusades in the name of "humanitarianism" or about "Christian patriots" who conflate nationalism with religion are especially important in a post 9/11 world. Events have proven Sheppard wrong about his belief that the threat to his generation posed by Nazi Germany, the Soviet Union, and Imperial Japan were inflated. But his claim that we too frequently create "bogey men" out of peoples, cultures, and ideas that are unfamiliar to us still rings true today. Sheppard's refusal to turn a blind eye to the moral perplexities that the pacifist necessarily confronts in a world in which innocent people often suffer at the hands of aggressors is a valuable reminder that applying moral commitments to real world situations calls for deep reflection, compassion, and humility. There's no easy recipe, nor is there call for smugness, when it comes to doing the right thing. Finally, Sheppard's vision of enlisting available media and international celebrities in the interest of peace has become a staple in the contemporary struggle for peace with justice. In so many ways, Sheppard anticipated the future in regards to both the obstacles to peace and the means to overcome them.

Today's Christian who reads *We Say NO!* is invited to reflect on what it means to be a disciple of Jesus in a violence-torn world. For Dick Sheppard, following Jesus meant honoring the Sermon on the Mount's recommendation of peacemaking, humility, compassion, and love, and this in turn meant that he didn't think a Christian could square war with his faith. He pitied the munitions factory worker, the physician, and the chaplain whose respective roles put them in the uncomfortable position of having to make hard decisions, and he refused to allow himself to judge them. But for his part, he was prepared to sacrifice his well-being and even his life in the service of the Prince of Peace. One story about him especially attests to the depth of his loyalty to the Christ who declared peacemakers blessed.

In writing about the Army of Peace that she, Herbert Gray, and Sheppard proposed in response to the 1932 Japanese invasion of Manchuria, Maude Royen remembered that many in Britain "thought the whole thing a mere theatrical gesture on our part." But she also recalled an incident that revealed as nothing else Sheppard's deep Christian commitment to pacifism. He had just declared his determination to personally lead the Army into Manchuria. Then, wrote Royden,

"*No Comfortable Business*"

> I shall never forget Dick Sheppard's words or tone when, realizing what his death must mean to those who depended on him materially or spiritually, Herbert Gray and I urged him not to volunteer himself. He went out of the room for a time and, when he came back, he said that he must go. He added, half under his breath, "The cup that my Father gave me shall I not drink it?"[32]

It was, concluded Royden, "this Christ-like" willingness on Sheppard's part to sacrifice himself for the sake of peace that drew thousands to his Peace Pledge Union, and led thousands more to respect his integrity even when they couldn't agree with his pacifism. Even three-quarters of a century after his death, Sheppard remains, and rightfully so, one of those non-martial heroes he hoped would inspire the rest of us to turn away from war. He knew all too well that following Christ the Peacemaker was "no comfortable business" in a world that accepted war as an inevitable fact of life. But his struggle to invite his contemporaries to think beyond conventional wisdom when it came to war clearly struck a responsive chord in thousands of them. To echo a prayer of Royden's, "May that conscience which Dick Sheppard awoke in his time never sleep again."[33]

A Note on the Text

This edition of Sheppard's *We Say NO! The Plain Man's Guide to Pacifism* for the most part follows the text of the original one published in 1935 by the London firm of John Murray. I've Americanized Sheppard's British spellings and supplied parenthetical chapter and verse to his many scriptural quotations, none of which he referenced himself, but I've left untouched his idiosyncratic capitalization as well as his exclusive use of masculine pronouns. The latter were the convention of his day, and changing them to be gender inclusive risks making his text cumbersome. For readers who are bothered by them (and I include myself in that category) it might help to know that Sheppard was a staunch proponent of women's rights, including ordination in the Church of England.

I've also tweaked the book's title. Sheppard's original title is *We Say "NO": The Plain Man's Guide to Pacifism*. But his *"NO,"* by virtue of its capitalization as well as the book's urgent tone, strikes me as clearly connoting

---

32. Royden, "Dick Sheppard: The Peacemaker," 78.
33. Ibid., 81.

NO!, and I've made the appropriate change. Textual purists, I hope, will forgive me.

All the footnotes throughout the text are mine. Many of them explain for the reader the historical references Sheppard makes in his text. Others provide bibliographical information about books he quotes. Following another convention of his day, Sheppard never supplied references to the many authors he cited. Whenever possible, I've tried to cite editions that Sheppard himself may well have read.

Kerry Walters

Major Works by H. R. L. Sheppard

The Human Parson. London: John Murray, 1924.

Two Days Before: Simple Thoughts about Our Lord on the Cross. London: SCM, 1924.

Fiery Grains (edited with H. P. Marshall). London: Longmans, Green, 1928.

The Impatience of a Parson. London: Hodder & Stoughton, 1927.

"Some Straightforward Issues," in *My Hopes and Fears for the Church*, 3–18. London: John Murray, 1930.

"Science and Religion," in *Science and Religion: A Symposium*, 83–92. London: Gerald Howe, 1931.

Echoes from St. Martin-in-the-Fields. London: Athenaeum, 1934.

If I Were Dictator. London: Methuen, 1935.

Sheppard's Pie (edited). London: Cassell, 1935.

Some of My Religion. London: Cassell, 1935.

We Say "NO": The Plain Man's Guide to Pacifism. London: John Murray, 1935.

My Cry for Christianity. London: Cassell, 1936.

God and My Neighbour. London: Cassell, 1937.

"Religion," in *The Root of the Matter*, 293–327. London: Cassell, 1937.

More Sheppard's Pie (edited). London: Cassell, 1938.

What Can We Believe? Letters Exchanged between Dick Sheppard and L. H. Edited by Laurence Housman. London: Jonathan Cape, 1939.

"No Comfortable Business"

The Best of Dick Sheppard. Edited by Halford E. Luccock. New York: Harper & Brothers, 1951.

Secondary Sources on H. R. L. Sheppard

The Peace Pledge Union website (www.ppu.org.uk) has links to some information about Sheppard. But except for an occasional mention in scholarly articles, no work, sadly, has been done on his life and writings for nearly a generation.

An Anonymous Member of the Peace Pledge Union. *H. R. L. Sheppard: A Note in Appreciation*. London: Cobden-Sanderson, 1937.

Matthews, Charles H. S. *Dick Sheppard: Man of Peace*. London: James Clarke, 1948.

Northcott, R. J. *Dick Sheppard and St. Martin's*. London: Longmans, Green, 1938.

Roberts, R. Ellis. *H. R. L. Sheppard: Life and Letters*. London: John Murray, 1942.

Scott, Carolyn. *Dick Sheppard: A Biography*. London: Hodder & Stoughton, 1977.

Various Authors. *Dick Sheppard: An Apostle of Brotherhood*. London: Chapman & Hall, 1938.

Various Authors. *Dick Sheppard, by His Friends*. London: Hodder & Stoughton, 1938.

Preface

THERE HAS NEVER BEEN a time in history when the desire for Peace has been so strong or so widespread as it is today. Throughout the world men and women are weary of war, and of the waste and suffering of war.

But, paradoxically, we live in imminent danger of a new and more terrible death struggle of the nations. The thing we hate and seek to avoid may yet overwhelm us.

That is because, while we are perfectly sincere in wanting Peace, we don't feel quite so sure of the other fellow's sincerity when he says he wants it too. So we are trying to build up a Peace system on the foundations of force, and hedging it round with military sanctions.

I do not believe that Peace can be established on such a basis. I am afraid that collective security may, in the end, prove a short cut to universal war.

Yet I do not despair. I believe that the world will to Peace may yet be made effective. But this can only happen if we renounce war, not only formally, but absolutely and unconditionally.

I want all the nations to do that. I believe that they would, if only one of the Great Powers had the faith and courage to lead the way. I want Britain to be that Power, and I want her to show that she is in earnest by disarming completely.

Now, this seems a 'tall order." It is probably true that no Government would dare to take the "risks" of disarmament unless it were convinced that such was the popular will, that the great mass of thinking men and women in the country demanded it. But I believe that politicians generally underestimate the strength of the Peace Movement, and that the general public is ready to accept very drastic measures if they offer a real hope of the abolition of war.

In order to test this feeling, and to give Pacifist opinion a chance to crystallize, I launched my Peace Pledge, and invited individual men to sign

Preface

an undertaking that they would have no part or lot in any future war. I have written this book in order to explain that Pledge, and to put before my countrymen the reasons why I consider it necessary. I have also tried to show why, in my opinion, those people are mistaken who, earnestly desiring Peace, believe that it can be secured by systems of collective security.

I may be told that I am a visionary, and that I am ignoring the facts of the international situation and of human nature. The facts of the international situation are not fixed and immutable. They would be transformed tomorrow if this country disarmed. The very existence here and elsewhere—similar pledges of non-participation in war have been signed extensively in the United States[1]—of large numbers of declared Pacifists is one of the facts of the international situation today. As to human nature, if it is natural to man to kill, it is surely more natural to kill a personal enemy, in the heat of passion, than to slaughter in cold blood someone against whom one has no grievance whatsoever. Yet we have been successful, in every civilized country, in discouraging the killing of personal enemies.

Pacifism seems to me to be common sense. But I believe that war is not merely foolish, it is also wicked. This book has been written primarily from the standpoint of the Christian, who holds that war is contrary to the spirit and teaching of Our Lord.

I am aware that many good Christians, while they abhor war, consider that it may yet be permissible and even necessary in certain circumstances. I have endeavored in these pages to convince them of their error.

One final word. Those associated with the League of Nations Union and the Peace Ballot, or who support the partial systems of collective security embodied in the Pacts, may consider that I have been less than just to their genuine desire for Peace.[2] The more strongly they feel that, the greater are

---

1. See chapter VI.

2. The League of Nations Union (LNU), founded in 1918 immediately after the end of World War I, was a British peace organization inspired by the formation of the League of Nations. Its guiding conviction was that international justice and peace were necessarily founded on the "collective security" that comes from international treaties that build military alliances. At its peak, the LNU had nearly a half million members. The Peace Ballot was a LNU-sponsored national survey, conducted in late 1935 and early 1936, that asked respondents a series of questions gauging their commitment to the League of Nations' internationalist vision. Thirty-eight percent of the adult population participated in the survey. The result was an overwhelming endorsement of Britain's membership in the League of Nations, international disarmament, international prohibition of for-profit arms sales, and international cooperation to forestall or stop aggression. The irony, as Sheppard saw it, was that the very principle of collective security endorsed by the LNU

Preface

the reasons why they should ask themselves: "Are we being similarly unjust to those other people whose will to Peace we doubt, and against whose possible aggression we are trying to guard? And may they not be similarly suspicious of us? And if so, is there not something in the arguments of this book after all?" It would be indeed one of the most tragic blunders in history if a world, passionately desiring Peace, drifted again into war because no nation would believe in the honesty of the others, because every nation was afraid of its neighbors. But that blunder is all too possible if we continue to rely on the sanctions of force.

H. R. L. S.

---

created military alliances similar to the ones that led to the First World War.

I

Twenty-One Years After

In September 1914 I knelt by a dying soldier. I had just arrived in France. He was the first soldier I saw die.

As I bent to catch his painfully spoken words I discovered that he had little need of my ministry. He was thinking of a life that was still unborn. His wife was expecting a baby about Christmas. And he died thanking God that, if the child was a boy, he would never have to go through the hell of war.

I learned from what the man said that his home was in the East End of London, but I could not ascertain his name. They were too busy where I was to bother about names. So I have never been able to find out if the child was born, and if it was a boy.

That man believed what he had been told—that he was fighting in the war to end war. Innumerable others also believed it and died, as he did, at least happy in the thought that their sons would be spared their Calvary.

These sons are of military age today.

The eleventh of November, 1918.[1] I had heard of the Armistice in advance, just in time to get handbills printed and distributed, inviting all who cared to do so to come to St. Martin-in-the-Fields.

For twenty-four hours we had service after service. We sang simply hymns, offered up simple prayers of thanksgiving. We poured out our hearts in gratitude to God, not so much because He had given us the victory, not

---

1. The ceasefire which signaled the end of World War I, took effect at 11 a.m. on the eleventh day of the eleventh month. It is commemorated in England each November 11 as Remembrance Day with a ceremony at the Cenotaph monument in Whitehall, not far from Sheppard's church of St. Martin-in-the-Fields.

even because at long last the killing was over, but because there would be no more war.

And today the nations are arming. Twenty-one years after the outbreak of war, seventeen years after the Armistice, the skies are dark once more.

We gave thanks to God that there would be no more war, but we wanted Peace without being willing to pay its price. It is our fault that the world trembles once more on the brink of the madness of blood.

It is our fault—the fault of Christian men and women in all nations, but especially of Christian men, because we have been unwilling to accept the practical implications of our Christianity. Our faith has been a shadow, not a flame. We have worshipped God for an hour or so on Sunday, and tried to safeguard the rest of the week by means of a "gentlemen's agreement" with the Devil. So we have won the Peace that we deserve—a Peace precariously poised upon the points of bayonets.

Peace cannot depend on armaments. It cannot be preserved by force. It cannot be organized, any more than Love can be organized.

We all know that in our hearts. But we have been afraid to act upon that knowledge. "It is not our business," we have said. "We have given the politicians a mandate—they know that we want peace, that another war would mean the end of civilization. It is their job, not ours, to see that Peace is maintained, that war does not come again. And they also want Peace. They have told us so, over and over again, in their speeches. Surely we can leave it to them."

Well, we have left it to them. And they have given us mechanized armies, squadrons of battle planes that darken the sun, bigger and better bombs, more lethal poison gas. God help the Peace that rests on such foundations!

But the fault is not the politicians'. It is our own. I believe that the great majority of the world's statesmen sincerely want Peace. But they are still hypnotized by that Devil's paradox: "If you want Peace, prepare for war."[2] They believe in a Peace of penalties—that if only war can be made sufficiently terrible, it will never happen. That a system of Pacts and understanding, which make war automatic in certain eventualities, will prevent these eventualities arising.

I can see their point of view. Their arguments are specious enough. And perhaps, for five, or ten, or twenty years, they will be able to slide from

---

2. *Igitur qui desiderat pacem, praeparet bellum*, often attributed to the fifth-century *De re militari*, a military manual written by one Vegetius, popular from late Antiquity to the Middle Ages.

crisis to crisis, and still stave off the evil day. But it may come suddenly—like a thunderblast.

They know that. But so long as they place "security" before Peace, national interest, national prestige before Peace, they can do no other. They are doing their duty according to their lights.

I do not propose to attack the politicians. I give them every credit for sincerity. They are probably far wiser than I am. But the wisdom of this world is foolishness with God, and I am God's servant, pledged to obey His word. I believe that, at this time, a special responsibility rests upon all individual Christians and upon the Christian Churches. I believe that the world is drifting towards war largely because we have not had the courage of our Christianity, and that, even at the eleventh hour, we may yet transform the situation if we forget all that we have been told about "practical politics" and try instead a little practical religion.

The dangers that the politicians see are real. They are trying to guard against them by measures which seem to them wise and prudent. Let us assume, for the moment, that they are wise and prudent—that, in fact, in the circumstances of today, they are taking the best, and perhaps the only course that is open to them.

That does not affect our duty as Christians in the least. It only makes it more urgent. We have to change those circumstances.

We can do that by stating the Christian attitude towards war, the attitude that is crystallized in the words of the Commandment, "Thou shalt not kill!"

Suppose that the Christian Churches in this country discovered that Commandment, and stated it, and said quite simply that the words meant exactly what they said, and all the flags and the drums and the bugles in the world could not alter or modify them one jot or tittle.

Suppose that all the individual Christians in this country did the same—and pledged themselves publicly, bound themselves by a solemn undertaking that they would have no part or lot in any future war, that no matter what the circumstances of that war might be, they would not take up arms.

Suppose, in short, that we took God's word seriously, that we decided He meant what He said, and resolved to obey Him.

Do you think that would have no effect? Don't you think that it would change the circumstances in which the politicians had to act and make their plans? Of course it would. They would be forced to try to find some other method of preserving Peace than armaments and Pacts of mutual assistance, which mean, in effect, agreements to fight.

But other countries . . . ?

Have you ever noticed that, whenever you are involved in a road accident, however slight, it is always the other man who is at fault? That whenever anyone is involved in a road accident it is always the other man who is at fault?

We'd all be safe drivers, and never have any sort of trouble, if there were nobody else on the highway. And everything would go smoothly at home and in business, if it weren't for other people.

But—have you ever tried meeting these other people halfway? It's wonderful how quickly most of them respond.

Those other nations of whom we're so much afraid consist of men and women like ourselves. They respond just as we do to "the decent thing," to an act of trust. They're just as good Christians as we are. Don't you think they'd be interested in some millions of people deciding that Christianity and war were incompatible and that, at whatever cost to themselves, they must be true to Christ? Don't you think that they might be forced to do some thinking of their own about war in the light of this strange new phenomenon?

And the moment people really think about war, instead of taking it for granted as a necessary evil, that moment war is finished.

Then there are the Churches. If the Christian Churches in this country took the line I have suggested, do you think that the rest of the Christian Churches throughout the world would remain silent? They would commit spiritual suicide if they did.

All very fine and large, you say, but I am forgetting about the Dictatorships.

They are very powerful, these Dictatorships, but their rule rests, in the last analysis, upon the consent of those they govern. And have you noticed what happens when a Dictator invades the sphere of religion, and tries to assert his secular authority in spiritual affairs?

The most remarkable, and the most hopeful, thing in the world today is the way in which, under Dictatorships, religion is finding its feet, Christianity is once more becoming a reality, and not merely an empty form, to those who profess it.

Even of the Dictatorships we need not despair.

But suppose I am unduly optimistic, suppose that we in this country pledge ourselves that never again shall we take part, in any circumstances, in war, and that our action awakens no answering echo in other lands.

Suppose that the other Christian Churches of the world remain silent, that all the individual Christians in other lands merely shrug their shoulders, mutter something about "these mad English," and make no attempt to follow the lead we have given.

Suppose that some Great Power, covetous of our wealth and possessions, takes advantage of our unarmed state, our pledge of non-resistance, to declare war upon us. Suppose we lose, one by one, our Dominions and Colonies overseas and that an enemy invades our shore.

Does that mean that war is right, or that we were wrong when we decided to obey God's Commandment, "Thou shalt not kill?"

Right and wrong aren't fluid. The moral quality of an action doesn't depend on its results.

The fact that I may gain a personal advantage by stealing doesn't make it morally right for me to do so. Even if I stole from people who wouldn't miss the money and handed over the proceeds of my crime to the unemployed, it still wouldn't be morally right.

Still less could I justify killing a man, though I might think that the world would be a better place without him.

Does it make any real difference to the moral quality of this action of killing if I put on uniform to do it, and if the majority of my fellow countrymen consider it praiseworthy? I can't honestly think that it does. I have to answer to my conscience for what I do, and my conscience can't get beyond that injunction, "Thou shalt not kill!"

I believe that, to a certain extent, even the politicians are beginning to realize that. But they can't conceive of a world without war. They want Peace themselves, but they can't credit the statesmen of other countries with wanting it too. And they're convinced it's their duty to prepare for a new and greater Armageddon. So they're up against a double problem. How to increase armaments without alarming the public. And how, when war comes, to dope the consciences of those they send out to slaughter, so that they won't have those inconvenient qualms about killing people.

So we are being told that the only real hope of Peace is to establish a system of Pacts or guarantees, which will automatically bring this country into any future European War. In case we're called upon to fulfill our obligations, we must have armaments. But there's nothing militaristic about these armaments, because their only purpose is to maintain Peace.

Naturally, the statesmen hope that the armaments won't be required—that the Pacts will really prevent war, at least for a time. But I doubt whether any of them really believes that they will give us permanent Peace.

That, in a nutshell, is the position today. In the name of International Cooperation we are being jockeyed into a position in which, sooner or later, war is practically inevitable. Twenty-one years ago, we entered the War to End War. Now we are preparing for the War to Preserve Peace.

I am writing this book to describe what I believe to be the better way—the only way which the Christian can conscientiously take. I am writing it to express not only my own views, but the views of the thousands who have signed the Peace Pledge with me. I am writing it to commend that Peace Pledge to all who profess the religion of Jesus Christ, and to the Christian Churches. I am writing it also for those who, without being attached to any religious organization, and while unable to accept the Divinity of Christ, still recognize in His teaching the highest standard of thought and conduct that has ever been given to the world. I am writing it for all who believe in "something, not ourselves, that makes for righteousness,"[3] for all to whom right and wrong are living forces and not dead abstractions of metaphysics. I am writing it for all men and women of good will.

And the pity is that, twenty-one years after 1914, such a book should be necessary.

---

3. A paraphrase of Matthew Arnold's minimalist definition of God as "an enduring power, not ourselves, which makes for righteousness" (In *Literature and Dogma* (New York: Macmillan, 1873) 331).

II

Christ and the War-Mongers

I REMEMBER ONCE LISTENING to a brilliant monologue against Christianity. It was in the days before I had ever even considered Ordination, and I must admit that I was greatly impressed. So were the other young men who were present—we all listened intently to the vibrant, passionate words of the arraignment.

The wars for which Christianity had been responsible—the persecutions, the burnings, the torturings—all the long, sad story of "man's inhumanity to man" for close on 2,000 years. Smiling fields turned into desert, homes made desolate, millions of lives cut short in their fairest morning hour.

"And this is Christianity!" the speaker concluded, his voice ringing with scorn.

A man who had been sitting quietly in a corner looked up.

"That isn't Christianity," he said; "that is the lack of it."

The spell was broken—the brilliant bubble pricked.

I wish it were as easy to prick that other bubble of Christian militarism—to break the spell which still persuades so many sincerely devout men and women that, even if war in the abstract is evil, some wars may be necessary and right.

In my first chapter I assumed that war is always wrong, that it is contrary to the spirit and teaching of Christianity. But even while I did that I knew that many people would disagree, that there were thousands upon thousands of good Christians who would immediately say: "But this isn't

Christianity as I understand it. There's nothing in the Bible that makes patriotism a sin."

Let us get this straight at once. It is fundamental. And never mind how the Churches interpret Christ's words; let us go back to those words themselves!

"Right," say our Christian patriots. "But you mustn't pick and choose. You must take the Bible as a whole, and remember the Old Testament as well as the New. What about the wars of the Jews against the Philistines, wars waged under Divine orders? And even in the New Testament there are passages—."

It is a curious thing how often those who say that you mustn't pick and choose in the Bible do so themselves. And you will notice how the Christian who seeks to justify war doesn't want to take Christ as his first authority. He feels instinctively he is on surer ground with the Books of Joshua and Judges and Samuel, and only selects what, in the teachings of Our Lord, he thinks will suit his purpose.

However, we'll take the Old Testament. We find there the Ten Commandments, and one of them is, quite unequivocally, "Thou shalt not kill."

But that has to be read in relation to the whole of the Old Testament background? It doesn't refer to killing in wartime, when to slay the enemies of our country becomes a patriotic duty? The Jews weren't really breaking the Commandment when they overran the land of Canaan with fire and sword? They were doing God's will?

Is this what the Christian patriot is thinking? We are justified in killing our enemies in war because the Jews killed theirs and their campaigns are recorded in the Old Testament? On that logic we need have no qualms about killing women and little children because Joshua, at the taking of Jericho, "utterly destroyed all that was in the city, both man and woman, young and old"; and "smote all the country of the hills, and of the south, and of the vale, and of the springs, and all their kinds; he left none remaining, but utterly destroyed all that breathed, as the Lord God of Israel commanded" (Josh 6:21; 10:40).

The Christian patriot protests; Joshua was a little too enthusiastic. No one wants to hurt women and children. After all, we must have a sense of proportion. The Jews of those days weren't so civilized as we are; they didn't have our advantages.

Well, even a Christian patriot should be a little more consistent than that. Besides, he is unwise, if he really believes that war can be justified, to throw Joshua overboard so precipitately. For large numbers of women and children were, in fact, killed in the last war, and infinitely more will be killed in the next.

"The moment another war starts, I'm going to join up," an ex-soldier said to me recently. "I reckon the safest place will be in the front line trenches."

I don't know how safe the front line trenches will be. But I do know that no town or city in any of the belligerent countries will be safe. I know that death will rain from the skies, and that, in the shambles that will be London or Manchester, Paris or Marseilles, Berlin or Munich, Rome or Milan, there will be no distinction of age or sex.

You cannot expect chivalry from a bomb. The fiercest of the ancient Israelites was more pitiful than poison gas.

So the Christian patriot needs those passages in the Old Testament that justify the slaughter of women and children. Modern warfare involves that, and on a larger scale than ever those warriors of old dreamed of. And those other passages that relate how the dead were mutilated (cf. 1 Sam 17:51 and 31:9)—the Christian patriot must accept them also. War today means mutilation, both of the living and the dead.

Please don't think I am making debating points. This is far too serious for that. I am simply trying to drive home what War means. It is back now at exactly the point where it was when the Israelites came into Canaan. It is a struggle of populations. There is no restriction on massacre; no close season for non-combatants. The only difference is that the scale is immeasurably larger—we have nations instead of tribes—and the technique of slaughter has been improved out of all recognition.

So, when you go to the Old Testament to justify war, you are not finding excuses for the charge of the Light Brigade, or the Thin Red Line, or Sir Richard Grenville's last fight, or any other heroic and colorful episode in history.[1] You are finding excuses for all the cruelties of Joshua's campaigns, plus the blind horror of the new scientific warfare.

And, in any case, is the Old Testament a reliable guide to conduct in the modern world? If it were, those of us who could afford it would

---

1. The charge of the Light Brigade and the stand of the "Thin Red Line" refer to events during the Crimean War's Battle of Balaclava on 25 October 1854. In the first, made famous by Alfred Lord Tennyson's poem, British light cavalry made a courageous but tragic frontal assault on Russian artillery. In the second, a regiment of red-coated Highlanders held off a Russian cavalry charge. Sir Richard Grenville (1542–1591) English sea captain, explorer, and national hero, was mortally wounded at the Battle of Flores while fighting against overwhelming odds.

be permitted to have as many wives and concubines as Solomon (1 Kgs 11:3) and "stubborn and rebellious" sons would be stoned to death (Deut 21:18–21).

But need I go on? We all know—even the Christian patriot knows—that the Old Testament requires to be interpreted in the light of the New. But there are certain passages in the New upon which, as I have mentioned, the defender of war relies. Taken in conjunction with the historical books of the Old Testament, they constitute his case that warfare is not necessarily un-Christian.

Some of these passages are sayings of Our Lord.

In the Gospel According to St. Luke, Christ is represented as saying: "When a strong man armed keepeth his palace, his goods are in peace" (Luke 11:21).

Matthew, Mark and Luke all quote Him in almost identically the same words: "Render unto Caesar the things that are Caesar's; and unto God the things that are God's" (Matt 22:21; Mark 12:17; Luke 20:25).

And when He sent out the Twelve Apostles to preach, He said, "Think not that I am come to send peace on earth: I came not to send peace, but a sword" (Matt 10:34).

In his admirable book, *Peace with Honor*, Mr. A. A. Milne has examined the first two of these texts. He points out that the sentence about the "strong man armed" is followed by another: "But when a stronger than he shall come upon him, and overcome him, he taketh from him all his armor wherein he trusted, and divideth his spoils" (Luke 11:22).[2]

Now, it might be thought that the first sentence of these two justified "preparedness," and the second the Treaty of Versailles.[3] But is not the essential thought the same as that which Our Lord expressed elsewhere: "All they that take the sword shall perish with the sword"? (Matt 26:52).

If history has any lesson for mankind it is surely this, that while force may keep a nation's goods in peace for a time, in the long run "a stronger" always arises. Where are the Empires of yesteryear? Mussolini rules in Rome, but it is no longer the Rome of the Caesars, drawing tribute from the ends of the earth. Spain has had her hour, and France—and it is all

---

2. A. A. Milne, *Peace with Honor* (New York: E. P. Dutton, 1934) 84.

3. The peace settlement at the end of World War I imposing penalties against Germany that included near total disarmament, financial reparations, and territorial concessions. Many observers believed the penalties too harsh.

as a dream that has passed. And how much of old dominion—how many conquerors and kings—have been blotted out by the sands of the desert?

I hardly think it is necessary for Mr. Milne to explain that, in the context from which these sentences were taken, Christ was talking of the casting-out of devils. We can afford to take the words at their face value, as they stand. They warn us that, if we trust in force, it will fail us in the end.

"Render unto Caesar . . ." "The interesting thing about these words of Christ's," says Mr. Milne, "is that they were not said to the Romans but to the Jews; and the Jews were a conquered race."[4] Our Lord is preaching non-resistance; submission to authority even when that authority is founded on usurpation or conquest and exercised unjustly or capriciously.

National pride revolts at the idea of tame submission to an alien yoke, and the Jews were a stiff-necked people. They liked Roman rule as little as we should like German. But Christ cared nothing for national pride. In effect, He told this people, with its long tradition of warfare, its faith in Jehovah as the God of Battles, that their land was now a Roman province, and they must accept the fact.

But it is one thing to submit to injustice patiently, and another to become active doers of evil. So Our Lord made it quite clear that there were limits to the obedience which could properly be given to authority. "Render unto Caesar the things which are Caesar's; and unto God the things that are God's." A man must obey the Powers that be even when it is against his interest or hurtful to his pride to do so; but he must not obey them against his conscience.

So this text, so often quoted in support of the claim of the State to make soldiers of its citizens if it considers it necessary, in reality has precisely the opposite effect. If war is morally wrong, if it is contrary to the teachings of Christ, we are no more entitled to engage in it than we are to worship idols or to commit adultery. And no orders which we receive from authority can alter our personal responsibility in the slightest.

In such circumstances, what does "Render unto Caesar the things which are Caesar's" mean? Simply that, if our rulers go to war, we are not entitled to try to stop the war by force. Revolution is ruled out, even if its object is to restore Peace. and if, in the event of war, we are sent to prison as conscientious objectors, we must not resist the officers who arrest us. We must "go quietly."

---

4. Milne, *Peace with Honor*, 85.

We Say NO!

This is not quite so one-sided as it sounds. I hope and believe that, if another war breaks out, there will not be enough prisons to accommodate all the conscientious objectors who will refuse service in the Forces.

Now we come to the third quotation. We may regard it as a prophecy; as a plain statement of the fact that misconceptions of Christianity would lead to wars of religion, persecutions, martyrdoms. That has indeed been the case. You remember Swinburne's passionate lines:

> Face loved of little children long ago,
> Head hated of the priests and rulers then ...
> Say, was not this thy Passion, to foreknow
> In death's worst hour the works of Christian men?[5]

They are all too true.

But if we suggest this interpretation, we are making an unnecessary concession to the Christian patriot. We are accepting, as he does, that the words refer to war. They don't. We will ask the Christian patriot to read on. Our Lord continues:

"For I am come to set a man at variance against his father, and the daughter against her mother, and the daughter in law against her mother in law.

"And a man's foes shall be they of his own household.

"He that loveth father or mother more than me is not worthy of me: and he that loveth son or daughter more than me is not worthy of me ...

"He that findeth his life shall lose it: and he that loseth his life for my sake shall find it" (Matt 10:35–38).

Christ was thus warning His disciples of the difficulties which all who embraced His teaching would meet in their own homes. New ideas are explosive in their effects. Those who accept them are, all too often, condemned to loneliness and misunderstanding. Their parents cannot understand why a promising career should be sacrificed to "impracticable idealism." Their wives say: "But you have a duty to me. Suppose you lose your job because of this nonsense. You're not entitled to take risks like that. And what are all my friends going to think?" or, a little later: "Other women get new clothes. Their homes look nice. These crazy ideas of yours are impossible. Look what they've reduced me to! I haven't a rag to my back. And look at that shabby carpet! And the whole place needs to be redecorated. And I'm sick

---

5. In his 1882 poem "On the Russian Persecution of the Jews," Algernon Charles Swinburne (1837–1909) laments that self-professed "Christian men" launch pogroms in the name of their religion.

of that old furniture! Everybody is sorry for me, married to you, and you don't know how humiliating that is to a woman. But of course you don't care. You don't love me anymore. You can't, or you wouldn't go on like that."

It's difficult to fight against that sort of thing. And a man's own heart will whisper to him: "It is rough on her, you know, and, after all, she is your wife. You promised to comfort and honor her, love her and cherish her." Or, more insidious still, it will say: "It doesn't matter about us, but there are the kiddies. They're entitled to their chance, and they won't get it if this goes on. I don't know how I'm going to be able to educate them properly, I don't even know how I'm going to clothe them decently, or how long they'll have enough to eat. And they don't understand—they can't understand."

I sometimes think that it must have been harder for the early Christians to overcome these insidious foes of their own household, who appealed so strongly to their natural affections, than it was to defy the stones and scourges of their persecutors, the devouring flames and the wild beasts of the arena. But Christ was quite definite—the sacrifice had to be made. Duty to God must come before duty to family.

All this has only a historical interest to the Christian patriot. But let him think for a moment of his own attitude to the man who refuses military service for conscience' sake, of the attitude of the modern State and general public opinion to such a man in wartime, and he may realize that these words of Our Lord's have a very personal application to the Christian who takes seriously the Commandment: "Thou shalt not kill."

And if, on further reflection, the Christian patriot should become convinced that war is contrary to the spirit of Christianity, then the passage becomes of vital importance to him. He started by using one isolated sentence in it as an excuse for his old attitude. Now he has to face the challenge of the whole.

But the Christian patriot, of course, is still unconvinced. He tries a new tack. He now switches over to St. Paul. If Christianity and war are incompatible, he says, why the insistence on military images in the writings of the Great Apostle? Why the idea of the Christian soldier?

For instance, in the Epistle to the Ephesians we find such phrases as "the whole armor of God," "the breastplate of righteousness," "the shield of faith," "the helmet of Salvation," and "the sword of the Spirit," and gather that St. Paul pictures the Christian as a fully equipped Roman legionary (Eph 6:14, 16, 17).

The Apostle used the phrases he thought best calculated to grip the imagination of those he was addressing, but did he therefore seek to justify war? In the very passage which exhorts us to "put on the whole armor of God" we find the following:

"For we wrestle not against flesh and blood, but against principalities, against powers, against the rulers of the darkness of this world, against spiritual wickedness in high places" (Eph 6:12).

Doesn't that describe, quite accurately, what the conscientious objector does when he refuses to bear arms?

And to emphasize the fact that here is no justification for militarism, we are told, still in the same passage, that our Christian soldier must have his "feet shod with the preparation of the gospel of peace" (Eph 6:15).

Or we turn to the Epistle to the Romans and we read:

"Bless them which persecute you: bless, and curse not . . ." (12:14).

"Recompense to no man evil for evil . . ." (12:17).

"If it be possible, as much as lieth in you, live peaceably with all men" (12:18).

"Dearly beloved, avenge not yourselves, but rather give place unto wrath: for it is written, Vengeance is mine; I will repay, saith the Lord" (12:19).

"Therefore if thine enemy hunger, feed him; if he thirst, give him drink: for in so doing thou shalt heap coals of fire on his head" (12:20).

"Be not overcome of evil, but overcome evil with good" (12:21).

I have known Christian patriots to read this passage and seize upon one sentence of it only: "If it be possible, as much as lieth in you, live peaceably with all men." But, they say, it isn't possible; the other people won't let us live peaceably with them.

They don't see that the responsibility is placed on us, not on the other people. "As much as lieth in you, live peaceably with all men." If we don't, it is because of some shortcoming, some failure in ourselves.

And now, what does Our Lord say? I quote from the Sermon on the Mount:

"Blessed are the peacemakers: for they shall be called the children of God . . ." (Matt 5:9).

"Ye have heard that it was said by them of old time, Thou shalt not kill; and whosoever shall kill shall be in danger of the judgment: But I say unto you, That whosoever is angry with his brother without a cause shall be in danger of the judgment . . ." (Matt 5:21–22).

"Ye have heard that it hath been said, An eye for an eye, and a tooth for a tooth: But I say unto you, That ye resist not evil: but whosoever shall smite thee on they right cheek, turn to him the other also . . ." (Matt 5:38–39).

"Ye have heard that it hath been said, Thou shalt love thy neighbor, and hate thine enemy. But I say unto you, Love your enemies, bless them that curse you, do good to them that hate you, and pray for them which despitefully use you, and persecute you . . ." (Matt 5:43–44).

"For if ye love them which love you, what reward have ye? Do not even the publicans do the same? And if ye salute your brethren only, what do ye more than others? Do not even the publicans so?" (Matt 5:46–47).

Can anyone, reading this, honestly say that war is permissible to the Christian? Only, I suggest, if he takes the view that religion is entirely divorced from citizenship. And Our Lord has something to say about that:

"No man can serve two masters: for either he will hate the one, and love the other; or else he will hold to the one, and despise the other. Ye cannot serve God and mammon" (Matt 6:24; Luke 16:13).

I remember hearing during the last war, that some official person had had the bright idea of suppressing a book written, I believe, by the late Bishop Gore on the Sermon on the Mount.[6] I remember, also, the indignant comment of a brother-chaplain:

"But how ridiculous! Everybody knows that sort of thing is purely academic. It has nothing to do with the war!"

I do not believe that Christ meant the Sermon on the Mount to be "purely academic." I do not believe that Christianity is "purely academic."

If it is, what is the good of it? If we do not accept Christ's words as a way of life, why pretend to hold them in reverence? Would it not be more honest to reject them altogether, to stop calling ourselves Christians?

Each of us must choose for himself. But I suggest that we should choose with our eyes open, not deluding ourselves. And the Christian attitude to war is exactly the same as the Christian attitude to sin. You know the story?

A man had come back from church, and his wife asked him what the sermon was about. "Sin," he replied. "Oh, and what had the minister to say about sin?" "He was against it."

No ingenious sophistry, no twisting of words and phrases, can alter the fact that Christ is against war, even when undertaken in defense against

---

6. Charles Gore (1853–1932) Bishop of Oxford, influential theologian, prolific author, founder of the Community of the Resurrection, and fierce critic of British imperialism.

aggression. Therefore the Christian must be against it. As Lowell wrote in the *Biglow Papers*:

> Ez fer war, I call it murder—
> There you hev it plain an' flat;
> I don't need to go no furder
> Than my Testyment fer that.[7]

The trouble is that we don't go to our Testament; or, if we do, the words are so familiar that we no longer bother about their meaning.

Otherwise there would be no such thing as a Christian patriot.

---

7. American poet James Russell Lowell (1819-1891) wrote two series of political satire entitled *The Biglow Papers*, the first during the Mexican War of 1846-48, the other during the Civil War. In the first series, the eponymous Hosea Biglow, writing in rustic Yankee dialect, inveighs against war and slavery. The verse quoted here is from the third English edition of *The Biglow Papers* (London: Trubner, 1861) 4.

III

Trying to Take in God

――― ―――

THE LAST CHAPTER ENDED with a quotation—or rather, part of a quotation—from the American poet, James Russell Lowell. After the four lines which declare that war is murder, he goes on:

> God hez sed so plump an' fairly
> It's ez long ez it is broad,
> An' you've gut to git up airly
> Ef you want to take in God.[1]

I have an uneasy feeling that this is exactly what a great many estimable people are trying to do today. They are trying to take in God.

We have already examined the position of the Christian patriot. But there is a more subtle—and perhaps more dangerous—patriotism which has appeared in the world during recent years. For want of a better name we may perhaps call it the patriotism of humanity.

Disraeli once wrote of "that great nation of nations, Humanity." In his day it was only a picturesque phrase. But there are now large numbers of people, in our own and other lands, who are endeavoring to make it a reality. They want to create an international super-State. They see in the League of Nations the nucleus of that World Community. They serve that idea as other people serve the land of their birth.

It is a lofty ideal. Those who hold it would say that there is nothing in common between it and the crudity of patriotism. I am reminded of the Temptation in the Wilderness.

1. James Russell Lowell, *The Biglow Papers* (London: Trubner, 1861) 4.

"The devil taketh him up into an exceeding high mountain, and sheweth him all the kingdoms of the world, and the glory of them;

"And saith unto him, All these things will I give thee, if thou wilt fall down and worship me.

"Then saith Jesus unto him, Get thee hence, Satan: for it is written, Thou shalt worship the Lord thy God, and him only shalt thou serve" (Matt 4:8–10).

Unfortunately, however, the answer of these League enthusiasts is not the one that Our Lord returned.

But what is the connection? The international idealists are genuinely puzzled. They want peace quite as much as we do. They are serving no national or selfish ends. And it is only in the World State that there can be realized the vision of the prophet: "The wolf and the lamb shall feed together, and the lion shall eat straw like the bullock . . . They shall not hurt nor destroy in all my holy mountain, saith the Lord" (Isa 65:25).

It sounds reasonable enough. Whatever conflict there may be between Christianity and patriotism, surely there can be none between Christianity and internationalism.

Wait a moment, however. What is the foundation on which this World State is to be built? Isn't it the same as the foundation of the national State—force? How is it to be established? In the same way as Empires usually are established. By force.

The dream of the World State is simply the old dream of World Empire in a new disguise. The Peace which it would establish would be only another *Pax Romana*—a Peace of the sword.

Absurd? Under the Protocol of 1924, which ardent League of Nations supporters still regret, each signatory State was to cooperate in defense of the League Covenant and in resistance to aggression "in the degree which its geographical position and its particular situation as regards armaments" allowed. War was declared illegal, unless—and this is the vital point—in cases where a nation was acting in self-defense, resisting an act of aggression, or *where it had taken up arms on behalf of the League against a recalcitrant State.*[2]

---

2. The Geneva Protocol for the Pacific Settlement of International Disputes, proposed to the League of Nations in 1924 by the British and French governments, was a scheme that called for compulsory World Court arbitration in disputes between sovereign states, disarmament, and military intervention by other League members as a final resort if arbitration fell through. The plan failed to receive full ratification by the League and was tabled.

Trying to Take in God

The Protocol was not adopted. The nations saw the shadow of the World Empire and recoiled from it. But since then we have had the series of Regional Pacts, beginning with Locarno, which may be said to go part of the way to the same objective.[3]

And the Jingoes of the League—World Empire has its Jingoism too—are still hankering after the ideas of the Protocol. Those who filled up the Peace Ballot, promoted by the League of Nations Union, will remember that one of the questions they were invited to answer was whether they were prepared to support the use of force against an aggressor.

In this theory—that force used against an aggressor by a combination of "law-abiding" nations is legitimate—and in the various Pacts, we have the basis of the "War to Preserve Peace" of which I spoke in the first chapter.

But, say our Internationalists, this is the only thing the practical peace lover can do in the circumstances of the modern world. We admit that, in certain eventualities, these Pacts and pledges mean war, but without them, war will be absolutely inevitable. They at least offer us a chance of avoiding it. We must take risks for peace.

How does Lowell put it?

> You've got to git up airly
> Ef you want to take in God.

If war is wrong, it doesn't matter whether it is embarked upon by a group of States, acting cooperatively to vindicate the League of Nations, or in accordance with the terms of a Pact. It is murder just the same. It is a crime against God and man.

We are too fond of drawing unreal distinctions. "I shall not take part in any Imperialist war," says the class-conscious proletarian. "But, of course, a war to overthrow capitalism—that would be quite a different thing." "I take a solemn pledge against all war," says the Internationalist, "except such wars as may be necessary to maintain Peace."

Both alike are deceiving themselves. And the Christians among the Internationalists are trying to take in God.

Let us look for a moment at the Pacts and the League. In effect, the Pacts are alliances.

---

3. The Locarno Pact, signed in 1925, was an agreement between Germany, France, and Belgium to respect one another's frontiers. The pact was guaranteed by Great Britain and Italy, but nullified eleven years later when Germany reoccupied the Rhineland, territory that she lost under the provisions of the Treaty of Versailles.

We Say NO!

"Not so," say the Internationalists; "under Locarno, for instance, we are bound to go to the assistance, not only of France, if she is attacked by Germany, but also of Germany, if she is attacked by France."

Imagine the outcry if France did attack Germany, and the British Government proposed to implement our obligations, and fight by the side of the Germans. There might very easily be a general strike to make our participation impossible—a general strike in which the great body of public opinion would be sympathetic to the T.U.C.[4] Why should we try to bolster up a Dictatorship, of whose methods and leaders we disapproved intensely? Why should we, for the sake of Herr Hitler, take up arms against one of the last of the Democracies of Europe?

If this is the case, Locarno is only an Anglo-French alliance in disguise.

Frankly, I do not believe in the Pact-makers. I cannot escape from the uneasy suspicion that every Power which signs a Pact does so with certain mental reservations, and that, when the time of test comes, the whole elaborate system of guarantees will break down. What we shall then get is not a group of nations combining against an aggressor, but two groups of nations arrayed against each other, and each prepared to advance irrefutable proof that there has been aggression by the other side.

The Pacts, in short, are not so much a contribution to Peace as a "cover" under which war may be prepared. They make expenditure on armaments respectable. A nation which has incurred obligations must put itself in a position to meet them. And when war comes, "the national honor demands that we redeem our bond."

But, the Internationalist objects, you're trying to have it both ways. You've just been saying that, if France invaded Germany, we'd throw Locarno overboard.

Have you ever heard of propaganda? Do you think that, in such a case, France wouldn't be able to justify her action by some story which would appear quite convincing to her own nationals and to every country that wanted to believe her?

We probably would end by meeting our obligations under the Locarno Treaty. But we would meet them by coming in on the side of France—because the real aggressor was Germany, and France had been forced, for reasons of self-preservation, to put herself "technically" in the wrong.

---

4. Trades Union Congress, the national federation of trade unions in the United Kingdom.

I am not in love with modern Germany, but I like war still less. And I want to make the Internationalist face up to the truth about these Pacts. When he thinks of our Locarno obligations, doesn't he always think of them in terms of security for France? Has he ever seriously visualized the situation with France as the invader of Germany? France wouldn't do such a thing? The Ruhr? Oh, there were exceptional circumstances in the case of the Ruhr.[5]

I want the Internationalist to realize that there always are "exceptional circumstances" to "justify" the invasion of one country by another. And that, in the case of every Pact, there are certain of the signatories who have common interests or sympathies, and who regard certain of the other signatories as natural rivals and enemies. The Pact is an insurance against these rivals or enemies. Thus there are formed groups within the Pact.

So far as practical peacemaking is concerned, therefore, I cannot honestly see that Pacts are any improvement upon alliances.

Much the same considerations apply in the case of the League of Nations. The League is, and can be, no better than the States which compose it, and whose official representatives sit in the Assembly or on the Council. Their jealousies, their suspicions, their fears dominate Geneva.[6]

There is much eloquence at the Assembly meetings. Tribute is paid, in many an impressive peroration, to idealism and international goodwill. But strip the speeches of flowery phrase and pious aspiration, and what do we find? Each of the orators is concerned only with the interests of his own country; none of them is prepared to make any real sacrifice for the good of the world as a whole.

But the League has never had a fair chance? If it had more power, if the member States were really prepared to support its decisions; if it had got proper backing, for instance about Manchuria—?

You see how again the idea of force appears. But if this did happen, can anyone doubt that in a relatively short time the League would be "run" by a little group of Great Powers who, because they supplied the fleets and the armies and the aircraft which imposed its will upon the world, would demand a dominant voice in its policies?

---

5. In 1923, France and Belgium seized the Ruhr, a mineral-rich region in Germany, in retaliation for Germany's defaulting on its war reparations. The occupation lasted for two years.

6. Geneva was the seat of the League of Nations' international headquarters.

That would mean World Empire, but not necessarily world peace. Empires have been rent by civil war before today. Some of the smaller Powers might rebel. The Great Powers might quarrel among themselves, and two formidable rival groups, each invoking the name of the League, fly at each other's throats in a cataclysmic strife.

The true Internationalist, however, wants an International force, under the League's own officers. All military aircraft, especially, would be under the League.

But is he sure that this might not, in the end, be even worse? He would be creating a "Praetorian Guard" which might develop along highly dangerous lines.

There is, in truth, no real security for world peace and good government under the League of Nations or any other system whose ultimate sanction is force.

An unnecessarily pessimistic conclusion, thinks the Internationalist. But my pessimism is easier to defend than his optimism. It is not many months ago since, in the opinion of the publicists, one of the main bulwarks of European peace was Signor Mussolini.

No doubt the Italian Dictator is a great man. Napoleon was a great man. Julius Caesar was a great man. But I can no more imagine Signor Mussolini as an angel of peace than I can visualize Napoleon or Caesar in that role. He himself, indeed, would indignantly deny that Peace had any place in his philosophy, except as a temporary expedient in particular circumstances. But let him speak for himself. In the statement of the philosophic basis of Fascism which he contributed in 1932 to the fourteenth volume of *Enciclopedia Italiana*, he wrote:

> And above all, Fascism, the more it considers and observes the future and the development of humanity quite apart from political considerations of the moment, believes neither in the possibility nor the utility of perpetual peace. It thus repudiates the doctrine of Pacifism—born of a renunciation of the struggle and an act of cowardice in the face of sacrifice.
>
> War along brings up to its highest tension all human energy and puts the stamp of nobility upon the peoples who have the courage to meet it. All other trials are substitutes, which never really put men into the position where they have to make the great decision—the alternative of life or death. Thus a doctrine which is founded upon this harmful postulate of peace is hostile to Fascism. And thus hostile to the spirit of Fascism, though accepted for what use they

can be in dealing with particular political situations, are all the international leagues and societies which, as history will show, can be scattered to the winds when once strong national feeling is aroused by any motive—sentimental, ideal, or practical.[7]

Honestly, what can we think of the prospects of European peace when one of its principal defenders writes in this vein?

The Internationalist replies: Yes, but that is only Mussolini's theory. In practice, he doesn't want war, any more than anyone else. And he's always very willing to cooperate.

So, if I remember rightly, was the Big Bad Wolf in Walt Disney's "Three Little Pigs." And there has been no pandering to the effete ideas of compromise and conciliation in Italy's dealings with Abyssinia.[8]

The Internationalist changes his ground. He suggests that, so long as some of the leaders of the nation holds views like Mussolini's, or are prepared to use the big stick as he has done, we've got to have Pacts or similar arrangements to safeguard ourselves, and to back up our adhesion to them by means of adequate armaments.

If I were asked to bet on a golf match, I don't think I would back the man who only played occasionally for the good of his health. I would feel that my money was safer on a man who played constantly, because he liked the game.

It's the same in most things. If you believe in war you have a much better chance of winning battles than if you are fighting unwillingly and half-heartedly.

If you don't believe in war—and our Internationalist says that he doesn't, except as a possible unpleasant necessity, in order to preserve peace—isn't it much more sensible to refuse to have anything whatever to do with it? You then oppose to the will to war of the Mussolinis of the world your own will to peace.

What good will that do? Well, the early Christians probably looked quite a lot at the armor-clad Roman soldiers, with their short swords and spears, and wondered what they could do against them. They certainly

---

7. The article, "*La dottrina del fascismo*" (pp. 847–51) although signed by Mussolini, was most likely ghostwritten by Giovanni Gentile (1875–1944) the self-styled "philosopher of fascism."

8. A reference to the colonial war brutally waged by fascist Italy against the Kingdom of Abyssinia in late 1935 and early 1936. The League of Nations was unable to prevent the invasion or to protect Abyssinia after it began, despite an eloquent plea to the assembly by Emperor Haile Selassie.

couldn't have done anything against them by fighting. If they had tried that, I'm afraid there would be no Christian Churches today.

Neither did they compromise. They didn't say to the Roman State: "We'll sacrifice at the altar of Mars, if you'll let us worship Christ as well."

The Roman State would have been willing to do that particular deal. They were quite prepared to add Christ to the Pantheon. One god more or less wouldn't have made any difference. Indeed, I believe that some such proposal was once actually made.

But these early Christians did really believe that they couldn't serve God and Mammon. They opposed to the many false idols the One True God. They opposed to the Roman idea of Power the Christian idea of Love. To the arrogance of the legionaries they opposed the meekness that endureth all things.

And they won. Down the centuries, it is true, there is much in the record of the Christian Churches that we might wish otherwise, but where they have failed they did so because they departed from the ideals and falsified the teaching of their Founder. But they have survived because of the strength of Christianity itself—because in every age, often in spite of the Churches, men have rediscovered the eternal truths that Christ taught by the shores of the Galilean Sea.

I commend that example to those who seek to establish world peace with the aid of tanks and battleships, bombing planes and submarines. They say that they must take risks for peace. There is only one risk that need be taken to make peace secure—the risk of disarmament. The Mussolinis worship courage—is there no statesman in the world with the courage to disband his country's soldiers and scrap its guns and war planes?

But I want to be quite fair. I know that while Governments seek to justify increases in armaments in the name of peace, by appealing to their obligations under international agreements, and there are many people who agree with them, there are many others who don't, who take a superficially different view.

Roughly, they say this: "We agree that to increase armaments is to betray the cause of peace. We criticize that just as strongly as you can possibly do. What we want and are working for is a system of pooled security within the League of Nations, and we accept the Pacts only as a first installment towards that. The nearer we approach the pooled security system, the more will it be possible for all the Powers to reduce their armaments. But because of the fears and jealousies and suspicions which do exist, we must give these guarantees of armed assistance in certain circumstances. Otherwise disarmament will never be attained."

That, I think, is the view of at least one of the great political parties. It may be taken as the view of the promoters of the Peace Ballot, and of the League of Nations Union.

I contend that there is only a superficial difference between that view and the attitude of those who make the Pacts an excuse for larger armaments. However much you reduce armies, navies and air forces, a skeleton war machine is left, and war is accepted as something which may, in a given situation, be necessary and right. Peace is still made to depend on force, or the fear of force.

This may be practical politics, but it isn't Christianity. If we honestly desire peace, I'm not sure that it is even practical politics. It is one of the peculiarities of modern warfare that a mere handful of men can spread devastation and death over a wide area. The skeleton force can be equipped, almost at a moment's notice, with practically limitless quantities of poison gas and high explosive. Factories can be changed over to the production of war material in a single night.

Also, the more armaments are reduced, the more efficient they become. Military, naval and air experts work overtime trying to make the smaller forces which are all they have left as formidable as the larger ones they formerly controlled. Less money may be spent on armaments; fewer men may be trained for war; but the menace still remains. Mars is not dead, but sleeping.

There is a further danger. So long as war remains a possibility, however remote; so long as it is accepted that, in a certain event, the use of force is justified, the temptation remains to appeal to its dread arbitrament "in a righteous cause."

For many years during last century the foreign policy of this country was in the hands of Lord Palmerston.[9] His strongest critic was John Bright.[10] Bright's sincerity in the cause of Peace is as much beyond doubt as that of any of those who today support pooled security as the only way to disarmament. One of the most moving and eloquent descriptions of the meaning of war in the language is that which fell from his lips in the House

9. Henry John Temple, 3rd Viscount Palmerston (1784–1865) twice prime minister of England. As foreign secretary, he became known for his policy of aggressive interventionism

10. John Bright (1811–1889) British radical member of Parliament and longtime opponent of England's imperialistic foreign policy.

of Commons at the time when our troops were fighting the Russian Army in the Crimea.

> The Angel of Death has been abroad throughout the land; you may almost hear the beating of his wings. There is no one, as when the first-born were slain of old, to sprinkle with blood the lintel and the two side-posts of our doors, that he may spare and pass on; he takes his victims from the cradle of the noble, the mansion of the wealthy, and the cottage of the poor and lowly.[11]

Yet it has been said that, if Bright had been in Palmerston's position, though we should not have had Palmerston's wars, we might have had Bright's wars.

That is probably an injustice to Bright, but there is a profound truth in it. So long as you retain, in any shape or form, the idea of war, while you make one single exception to the abhorrence in which you hold the slaughter of man by man; so long may the Pacifist of one day be the War Minister of the next.

At the time of the South African War Mr. Lloyd George braved hatred and violence to proclaim his opposition to this Imperialist adventure. But the Great War found him one of the most resolute and inflexible of all the Allied statesmen.[12]

Mr. Ramsay MacDonald opposed both the South African and the Great War. More than once he risked his life to carry the message of Peace to his fellow countrymen. The little band of those who tried to put a period to bloodshed looked to him as their leader and found inspiration in his unflinching courage.

Yet Mr. MacDonald, as Prime Minister, signed the White Paper which sought to justify an increase in British armaments, by arguments which, in the words of Mr. Atlee, made "the whole of his past career . . . futile folly."[13] Until we renounce war absolutely and without qualification or reserva-

---

11. John Bright, *Speeches on the Public Affairs of the Last Twenty Years* (London: Camden Hotten, 1869) 47. Bright's speech was delivered in the House of Commons on 23 February 1855.

12. David Lloyd George (1863–1945) was a vehement critic of the Boer War as a Liberal member of Parliament, insisting that the conflict was motivated by profit rather than the humanitarian reasons claimed by the government. But when he became Prime Minister in 1916 two years into the First World War, he became known as a ruthless hawk.

13. Ramsay MacDonald (1866–1937) was England's first Labor Prime Minister (1929–1935). Clement Atlee (1883–1967) was Labor Prime Minister from 1945–1951. The White Paper referred to by Sheppard was issued on 4 March 1934.

tion, there will always be circumstances in which even those who have most loved peace may feel it their duty to prepare for war, or even to go to war. And the more idealist we are, while war still retains a place in our philosophy, the greater is the danger that we may be impelled to make our country "the knight-errant of the human race," or at least of a part of it.

Take my own case. I abhor and abominate the persecution of the Jews in Germany. If I did not also abhor and abominate war, there might easily have been awakened an answering echo in my heart when Mr. Nathan Laski spoke on this subject at a Zionist conference in Manchester and said: "We are a scattered race who have no power to protect ourselves from persecution. Even small nations, such as the Belgians, the Greeks, and so on, are able to protect themselves internationally. If there had been similar persecutions among them as there is among the Jews there would have been war by now."[14]

Mr. Laski went on to refer to Gladstone's speeches on the Bulgarian atrocities.[15] Here again we had idealism sending out the fiery cross that calls to battle.

Even in a world of "pooled security," with armaments reduced to the minimum, there may be occasions which will make an equally powerful appeal to the emotions, and idealists who will deceive themselves into believing that here is just cause for war.

If these idealists are in control of government, then indeed we may have "Bright's wars."

That is why I am opposed to any peace system that is founded upon force, no matter how much reduced. Until we have turned all the swords into pruning hooks, until we have made up our minds that in no circumstances will we go to war, reasons for war will always be found, and wars will occur. And I believe that God's law forbids slaughter, and that we can't "take in God."

If you object that I am being unfair to the idealists, that they want peace as sincerely as I do, I can only reply that I admit it. But I wouldn't trust myself with the control of a war machine. And when I think of the

14. Nathan Laski (1893-1950) British Marxist, Labor Party leader, and professor at the London School of Economics.

15. The "Bulgarian atrocities" refers to the brutal Ottoman suppression in May and June 1876 of an uprising by Bulgarian subjects. An estimated 30,000 Bulgarians were slaughtered, prompting outcries from all over Europe. Gladstone, at the time between terms as British Prime Minister, protested the suppression in a number of speeches as well as a widely circulated pamphlet, "The Bulgarian Horrors and the Question of the East."

former Pacifists who are now justifying war preparations, I say to myself: "There, but for the grace of God, goes Dick Sheppard!" It is one of the ironies of history that Lowell, whose opposition to the Mexican War inspired the lines that I have quoted, lived to defend and justify a still more sanguinary struggle. The second series of the *Biglow Papers* was written to support the North in the fratricidal strife of the American Civil War.

IV

Inquest on John Brown's Body

AT THIS POINT I am going to make a digression. It will not please those who like books to be tidy, well-planned affairs, with no rough edges, no interruptions in the smooth flow of argument. But then I'm not writing for people like that. I'm writing for those to whom ideas, principles, truths are more important than the phrases in which they are dressed or the way they're presented.

And it has suddenly occurred to me that quite a number of my readers—men and women as honest and sincere as I am myself, and perhaps in many ways more able and skilled in discussion—are going to seize on what I've just written about Lowell and the American Civil War.

"Here," they will say, "was at least one war in which a Christian could fight with a clear conscience. And you can't say, when you think of this particular struggle, that force is always wrong, that it never accomplishes anything. This war freed the slaves!"

Well, let us have a look at this and other wars which are said to have been justified by their results. Let us see whether war has helped humanity to climb upward and onward—whether it has ever been worth its cost in human life and human suffering.

We are holding an inquest on "John Brown's Body"—trying to see whether the man who dies in arms, fighting in a quarrel which he believes to be just, and for no selfish ends, does help forward the cause he has at heart.

Let us take, first of all, the case of the American Civil War. To justify it, we must show not only that it did, in fact, lead to the freeing of the slaves, but that they could not otherwise have gained their liberty, and that the other results of the struggle did not outweigh the benefits of negro emancipation.

At the very outset of our investigation we make a curious discovery. This war was not waged in order to free the slaves. It was waged to prevent the Southern States seceding from the Union. But before Federal troops were launched against the Confederate South, efforts were made to find a compromise which would keep the seceding States under the Stars and Stripes. They were offered, among other things, an immutable amendment to the United States Constitution which would have perpetuated slavery.

Had this offer been accepted, American cotton would today still be grown by slave labor. And the offer was made because certain men, who wished to abolish slavery, had appealed to force in an attempt to advance their cause.

The Secessionist movement only became really serious after the Pottawatomie massacre, in which a number of pro-slavery farmers were murdered by Kansas Abolitionists, whose most prominent leader was John Brown, a former theological student whose deep religious fervor had been turned sour by hatred.

John Brown's was a one-track mind, and his faith, if strong, was also narrow. He was a man of the Old Testament, drawing his inspiration from Joshua rather than Christ. He saw himself as God's gunman, with a divine mission to slay the enemies of the Lord.

So Pottawatomie was followed by Harper's Ferry—and the South was in a blaze. Brown had planned a slaves' haven of refuge amid the Virginia mountains, a stronghold to which escaped slaves could flee, and where they would be able to defend themselves against their pursuers.

To obtain arms to make his scheme possible he led a raid on the Government arsenal at Harper's Ferry. It was successful, but before he could withdraw with the weapons he wanted, he was surrounded. After a desperate resistance, in which two of his sons were killed and Brown himself was badly wounded, he was captured. A trial followed. He was found guilty of treason, murder, and criminal conspiracy with slaves, and hanged.

Now, Brown died for the cause of the slaves. There is no doubt of that. And hundreds of thousands of Northerners hailed him as hero and martyr. But what had he accomplished? A number of men, including himself, were dead before their time—and the movement for secession had been given a tremendous impetus.

The Northern leaders were determined that, at all costs, the Southern States should be kept in the Union. So one of the first results of John Brown's efforts on behalf of the slaves was that the most solemn assurances were offered to the South that the "rights" of the slave owners should be respected.

In his first inaugural address as President of the United States, Lincoln repeated an undertaking which he had previously given.

"I have no purpose, directly or indirectly," he declared, "to interfere with the institution of slavery in the States where it exists. I believe I have no lawful right to do so, and I have no inclination to do so."[1]

He went on to promise that he would support the perpetuation of slavery by means of the immutable amendment to the Constitution already referred to.

God's gunman, by his appeal to violence, jeopardized the cause for which he cared most, for which he had been ready to die. As a result of his acts, the fetters might have been fixed more firmly than ever round the limbs of the American negroes, and the rising hopes of the Abolitionists have been shattered forever.

That, in itself, is an interesting commentary on the efficacy of force as an instrument of reform.

But the offer was refused, and the north took up arms in the words of Lincoln's first message to Congress, to maintain the "territorial integrity" of the Republic "against its own domestic foes."[2] And presently, as the Federal levies poured south to the battlefields they sang the most famous of war songs:

> John Brown's body lies a-mouldering in the grave,
> But his soul goes marching on!

Even then, however, the cause of the slaves had not been officially adopted. And, having regard to all the circumstances, perhaps we may be pardoned if we read a new meaning into the familiar lines. It was not the spirit of freedom and brotherhood that was marching on, but the spirit of violence and hatred. And half a million men were to follow the Kansas Abolitionist to the grave before peace returned to distracted America.

---

1. "First Inaugural Address—Final Text," in Roy P. Basler, ed., *The Collected Works of Abraham Lincoln* (New Brunswick, NJ: Rutgers University Press, 1953) 4:263. Lincoln delivered his inaugural address on 4 March 1861.

2. "Message to Congress in Special Session," in *The Collected Works of Abraham Lincoln*, 4:426. Lincoln's speech was delivered 4 July 1861.

True, after many hesitations, Lincoln did issue his Emancipation Proclamation. But can the lover of humanity feel altogether satisfied with its results? This act of elementary justice was a war measure, designed to weaken and embarrass the Confederate South. It was made effective by force. And the bitterness which it aroused, the fact that it was imposed on a defeated community, has poisoned relations between white men and black in America ever since.

The terrorism of the Ku Klux Klan, the mob murders of Lynch Law, the miscarriages of justice which so often occur when colored men are tried by Southern juries, the ostracism of those who have the faintest trace of negro blood, the intense racial animosities, which we in this country find so hard to understand—are they not the legacies of this war of seventy years ago?

Consider the state of the American negro today, think of the miseries which he constantly endures, the disabilities under which he labors, the relentless and vindictive savagery of which, at any moment, he may be a victim—and then tell me, if you dare, that it was worth five hundred thousand lives to produce this mockery of freedom!

Yet throughout American the South is noted for its chivalry. You can pay a man no higher compliment than to call him "a true Southern gentleman."

There is a poison in war. It makes the victors arrogant, overbearing, unjust. And it brutalizes the vanquished. Smarting under the sting of defeat, unable to avenge upon their authors the humiliations which they suffer, they yet must find an outlet for the hatred which consumes them.

We have seen that happen in Europe during recent years. We need look no further for the explanation of German Anti-Semitism. It is not true, as has been stated, that the German must always have someone to kick and, after the war, the Jew was the only person he could kick with impunity. The German is naturally decent and kindly. But defeat has bred strange fevers in his blood.

You may, if you like, talk of this in terms of modern psychology and call it an inferiority complex. The really important thing about it is not the name, but the fact that war almost invariably brings these grim consequences in its train. The defeated have to get right with themselves by taking it out on someone else. The Germans found the Jews at hand for this purpose; the Southern gentlemen had the negroes.

Might it not have been better, therefore, if another way had been found of freeing the slaves? Even if they had remained in bondage for a few more years, emancipation, when it did come, might have worn a fairer face. There was little advantage in exchanging the ship of the overseer for the lash of the Ku Klux Klan.

And there can be little doubt that a way to liberation would have been found. In a few more years, world opinion, and American sensitiveness to its verdict, would have compelled the adoption of some scheme which, while compensating the slave owners, would have put an end forever to the holding of property rights in human beings.

Lincoln, indeed, had such a solution in mind, and at one point in the struggle between North and South persuaded Congress to pass a resolution declaring that "the United States ought to cooperate with any State which may adopt a gradual abolishment of slavery" and promising compensation for the "inconveniences, public and private, produced by such change of system."[3]

Considered against this background, the American Civil War doesn't seem to have been such a good idea, after all. It got something done, but in an expensive and inefficient way. It reminds me of the Chinese in Lamb's essay who burned down their houses in order to eat roast pig, until "fuel and pigs grew enormously dear all over the district. The insurance offices one and all shut up shop. People built slighter and slighter every day, until it was feared that the very science of architecture would in no long time be lost to the world."[4]

The benefits of war, I am afraid, are usually of this doubtful kind. But we still await the coming of the sage who will convince us that we may have the equivalent of roast pig "without the necessity of consuming a whole house to dress it." And are we not still more absurd than Lamb's Chinese? They at least did not burn men and women and children as well as houses to get the meal they craved.

But perhaps you think that it is not enough just to examine one war? Very well, then, we will look at others. We will go back over history and select examples in which it is claimed, good has come out of the evil of slaughter.

Every schoolboy knows the name of Marathon and Salamis. In these two battles, and again, finally, at Plataea, the Greek city states repulsed the Persian invasion of Europe.

---

3. From a joint resolution of Congress, 11 April 1862, in *The Collected Works of Abraham Lincoln*, 5:146.

4. Charles Lamb, "A Dissertation upon Roast Pig," in *The Prose Works of Charles Lamb* (London: Edward Moxon, 1836) 2:280.

The struggle between Greeks and Persians was a war between liberty and despotism, progress and reaction. Had Darius and Xerxes been successful, we are sometimes told, democracy would have been strangled in its cradle, and the whole of world history would have been changed. There would have been no Western civilization, no Western philosophy, no Western culture, no Western science and invention, no gradual development of law and free institutions.

This is the accepted view. But, if we take it, are we to praise the Greeks for saving so much for future generations—or blame them for putting it all in peril? For it was the Greeks who began the war by helping the Ionian cities of Asia Minor in their revolt against Darius.

As a matter of sober fact, they neither endangered nor preserved so much.

"Had Darius won at Marathon or Xerxes at Plataea," writes the Warden of New College in the first volume of his monumental *History of Europe*, "it is difficult to believe that the free and distinctive life of the Greek cities would have suffered a final eclipse. Susa was far away, and to govern Greece from Susa would have exceeded the resources of any state of the ancient world. The Persians had already seen the wisdom of conferring some form of liberty on the conquered Ionian Greeks, and what was politic in Asia Minor was far more politic in Europe."[5]

Mr. Fisher, indeed, goes on to suggest that the marvelous flowering of Greek literature and art after Plataea was due to the exaltation of victory. This may be partly true, but I cannot believe that the hand of Pheidias would have lost its cunning, or Aeschylus and Sophocles refused to write had the fortune of war been otherwise. And I remember how the literature of the Jews was enriched by the Captivity.

Turning to another of the great wars of the ancient world, we find that Europe was again saved from Eastern domination by the triumph of the Roman arms against Carthage. That, at least, is the popular view. But it is just as inconceivable that Carthage could have Orientalized the West as that Persia could have done so. Not only was she handicapped in Imperialist adventures by civil strife at home, but there is evidence that she was more interested in commerce than in conquest. Also, she relied in her wars with Rome on the aid of Greek allies and Greek mercenaries, who, had she won, would have been in an enormously powerful position.

---

5. H. A. L. Fisher, *A History of Europe* (Boston: Houghton Mifflin, 1939) 31.

The apologists of war may be on stronger ground if they take not this one stage in the Roman path to Empire, but the whole story of Rome. Yet surely the world's debt to the city of the seven hills is not for the Roman wars, but for the Roman peace.

It was the supreme glory of Rome that she gave law to the world. And today, long centuries after the final dismemberment of the Empire, Roman jurisprudence remains. What was won by the sword fell to the sword, but all that was of permanent value in the achievement of the Roman spirit survived.

And now we come to a curious contradiction. The same people who claim that Western civilization was only saved from the dark tides of Oriental barbarism by the naval and military prowess, first of Greece and afterwards of Rome, also tell us that the Crusades were of immense benefit to Europe—because they brought its semi-barbarous peoples into contact with the civilization and culture of the East.

The Crusades did broaden European horizons. Our ancestors learned, under the brazen Syrian skies, something of Arabic medicine and chemistry. The efficient Arabic arithmetic ousted the clumsy Roman methods, impossibly handicapped by the alphabetical system of numeration. Geometry and algebra, kept alive by the Arab mathematicians, were rediscovered by the nations of the West. Trade with the East was opened up, and Oriental arts and crafts enriched the life of the rude Frankish lands.

There was an increased sense of the unity of Christendom, a quickening of interest in exploration and missionary enterprise. Some authorities also ascribe the first real advance in the status of European womanhood and the dawn of romantic love to the psychological changes brought about by this period of awakening and development. Men's minds began to shake off the shackles that had bound them. It would be no exaggeration to say that the seeds of Protestantism were sown amid the sands of Palestine.

These benefits were real, but how far could they be ascribed to war? So long as Crusaders and Saracens were endeavoring to kill each other on the battlefield, there was no possibility of anything of real value being learned by the one or taught by the other. But the strife was not continuous. There were periods of peace, during which Christians and Moslems lived side by side; the Franks who had settled in Syria formed friendships with Saracens, and imbibed something of their culture.

It is to these interludes that we owe all the good which came from the Crusades. Had the story of these years been exclusively of battles and sieges, Europe would have gained nothing from contact with the East.

True, it was war which brought the Franks to the Levant. But there had been peaceful settlement on a smaller scale before Peter the Hermit preached his Holy War.[6] I think, too, that the Italian merchants would have found their way to the Eastern markets even without the swords of the Crusaders to blaze the trail. It might have taken longer for the Arabic learning to filter through to France and Germany and England, but it would have done so in the end.

There is, however, another class of wars which we must investigate. Freedom of conscience is one of the supreme goods. And it has been dearly won. Authority's answer to the claims of individuals to worship God in their own way has filled the world's prisons and glutted its scaffolds. The wars of religion have drenched earth's fairest lands with blood.

Now we can see, quite clearly, how futile have been the attempts to stamp out ideas by force. But are we equally sure that no purpose has been served by the armed defense of ideas?

When the Dutch, for instance, defied the might of Imperial Spain—when England sent out her tiny ships against the Invincible Armada—did they not save Protestantism? And were the Puritans and Covenanters of a later period rebels against God as well as against the King when they asserted on the battlefield their right to interpret the Bible as their own hearts dictated?

History does not consist of a series of isolated incidents. We may or may not believe that it has a plan, a pattern, that events move towards some predestined end. But we cannot evade the fact that the present has its roots in the past, and that the words and deeds of men long dead come echoing down the halls of Time to mold the destinies of the living. We are not, indeed, the slaves of Yesterday. But we are its children. And however we protest against it we cannot entirely escape our inheritance.

We cannot therefore regard, for instance, the struggle of the Elizabethans against Spain as something which stands alone. We must recognize it as a link in a chain, and see what followed it.

From the defense of an idea by arms to the endeavor to impose an idea by the same means is only a step. The principle which England asserted against the Spaniards was that of the national, as opposed to the universal church—she set up, against the claim of the Pope to be the Vicar of God, the claim of the State to decide what its subjects should believe and how they should worship.

---

6. The priest (died 1115) whose preaching is credited with launching the First Crusade.

Now I believe that the Church of England was—and is—better adapted to satisfy the spiritual needs of the majority of our fellow countrymen than the Church of Rome. But it did not—and does not—possess a monopoly of religious truth. And there were, in that day as in this, many Englishmen who rejected certain articles of its creed and denied the authority of its Bishops.

God had scattered the Armada. He had answered the prayers of the faithful. He had shown that the Church of England was His Church, and that its enemies were His enemies. Why, then, should there be any toleration of those within the State who opposed themselves to the Will of God, thus clearly declared?

You see how powerful—and how natural—the argument was. And you see, because you know your history, where it led. But was there so much gain in defeating those who would have brought the Inquisition to our shores if the Star Chamber and High Commission Court were to harry men and women whom they considered heretics in a way scarcely less bigoted and cruel?

We triumphed against the emissaries of the Pope. But we proceeded to persecute those who refused to acknowledge the Archbishop of Canterbury. And they, in their turn, appealed to arms in defense of their faith and we had the Civil War.

It is to the eternal honor of Cromwell that, on the whole, he recognized liberty of conscience, and was prepared to tolerate views on religion other than his own. But that toleration was not extended to any creed which he considered dangerous to the State, and this, added to the fact that many of the Puritans were of a less accommodating temper, meant that persecution again raised its ugly head under the Protectorate.

In Scotland, bigotry assumed fantastic proportions. The people who praise the Covenanters for their spirited defense of liberty of conscience against the efforts of the successive Stuart Kings to establish Episcopacy should read the evidence on which Buckle bases his charge that, at the height of its power, the Scotch Kirk was "one of the most detestable tyrannies ever seen on the earth." He continues: "We may search history in vain for any institution which can compete with it, except the Spanish Inquisition. Between these two, there is a close and intimate analogy. Both were intolerant, both were cruel, both made war upon the finest parts of human nature, and both destroyed every vestige of religious freedom."[7]

---

7. Henry Thomas Buckle, *Introduction to the History of Civilization in England* (London: Routledge, 1904) 790.

I mentioned another of the great struggles for religious freedom—the war which led to the establishment of the Dutch Republic. Here also we find evidence of the evils that follow an appeal to force, even in a righteous cause. You may read in the pages of Motley how "human ingenuity to inflict human misery had not been exhausted in the chambers of the Blood Council" and "Reformers were capable of giving a lesson even to inquisitors in this diabolical science."[8]

It is true that Motley represents the atrocities of Sonoy as something entirely exceptional and unrepresentative, but it is impossible to explain away, as an unfortunate incident, the fate of the Remonstrants a few years later.[9] Here we had a band of men, some of whom had rendered distinguished service to the State, all of them honest and disinterested, hounded and harried because their particular brand of Protestantism was rather more liberal than the strict Calvinism of the Dutch ruling caste. Once again heretics were thrown into prison and men who had sought to overthrow a Catholic tyranny sent old comrades-in-arms to the scaffold because they held different views of the extent of God's mercy to mankind.

For twelve years the Remonstrants remained under the ban of the Dutch Republic before at last more Christian counsels prevailed and the "heretics" were allowed a measure of freedom.

There is another point worth noting in the story of the Netherlands. We think of the troubles of this period as a struggle between Protestants and Catholics and wax almost lyrical over the heroism of the Reformers, facing the most formidable odds in the name of religion. But for a long time, while Charles V was straining every nerve to extirpate Protestantism in the Netherlands with fire and sword, a large part of his army consisted of German Lutheran regiments, whose men regularly attended Divine service, conducted by their own Protestant chaplains, even while they helped to deliver their co-religionists to the torturers of the Inquisition and the executioners of the Emperor.

Only a few years before, the Germans had won religious freedom on the battlefield, and forced Charles to recognize their Protestantism in the

---

8. John Lothrop Motley, *The Rise of the Dutch Republic* (New York: Thomas Y. Crowell, 1901) 2:240.

9. Diederik Sonoy (1529–1597) a Protestant soldier in the Eighty Years' War (1568–1648) of Dutch independence from Spain. He defeated Spanish besiegers of the city of Alkmaar (1573) and afterwards conducted a savage reign of terror against Catholics. Remonstrants were liberal Protestant dissenters from orthodox Calvinism who endured persecution at the hands of Calvinist leaders in the Dutch Republic.

peace of Passau. There are few episodes in history more cynical than their employment, after these events, by the same Catholic ruler against their own Reformed religion in another part of his dominion. But what can we think of their willingness to be so employed?

This is perhaps an extreme example, but there is abundance of other evidence that those who fought in the wars of religion were not always those who took their faith most seriously. The greatest of all the Huguenot leaders in the strife that ravaged sixteenth-century France, the victor of Ivry, decided in the end that "Paris was worth a Mass." Montrose the covenanter became the most dreaded of all the enemies of the Covenant. William of Orange hesitated for long before he abandoned Catholicism for the Protestant communion. Richelieu supported the Reformers abroad while he fought against them in France. Cromwell and Mazarin found it expedient to be allies.[10] The incidents and exigencies of war and the statecraft which is based on war tend to blot out all else, even the causes for which, in the first place, the sword has been drawn. The Great War was a war in defense of democracy, but the democratic Powers had, as their ally, the most absolute ruler in Europe, the Tsar of All the Russias. And, as the struggle proceeded, the last vestiges of civil liberty were stripped away in their own lands.

This rule applies to every war and helps us to understand why force, even when used in defense of religious freedom, has hindered rather than helped the progress of mankind.

It is idle to say that, but for the fact that Protestants were willing to fight for their faith, Protestantism would have been blotted out.

"The Reformation broke out at least twenty times before Luther, and was put down," says Mill in his essay *On Liberty*. "Arnold of Brescia was put down. Fra Dolcino was put down. Savonarola was put down. The Albigeois

---

10. Henry IV (1553–1610) who converted from Protestantism to Catholicism as a condition for ascending the throne of France, is reputed to have quipped that "Paris was worth a mass." James Graham, 1st Marquess of Montrose (1612–1650) was a leader of the Scottish Covenanters, who rebelled against King Charles I of England when he attempted to impose Anglican worship on the Scots, but later switched his allegiance to Charles. William of Orange, although born a Protestant, converted to Catholicism as a young man to curry favor with Charles V, the Holy Roman Emperor. In 1568, when William led Holland in a rebellion against Philip II, Charles' son, he returned to Protestantism. Roman Catholic Cardinal Richelieu (1585–1642) First Minister to the King of France for nearly twenty years, often allied France with Protestant rulers during the Thirty Years' War when it suited France's interests. Oliver Cromwell (1599–1658) puritan Lord Protector of the Commonwealth, sent troops to assist Catholic France in its war with Spain. The French king's First Minister was Cardinal Mazarin (1602–1661) Richelieu's successor.

were put down. The Vaudois were put down. The Lollards were put down. The Hussites were put down."[11]

But always, though the Reformers died, their ideas reappeared. Sometimes—perhaps often—their deaths did more than their lives to spread their doctrine.

"Be of good comfort, Master Ridley," cried Latimer, as the flames crackled around the stake, "play the man: we shall this day light such a candle, by God's grace, in England, as I trust shall never be put out."[12]

Latimer had had no part in the conspiracies against Queen Mary; he had neither taken up arms against her nor encouraged others to do so. And his death was a thousand times more serviceable to his cause than if he had perished on the battlefield. He won back all, and more than all, that the violence of others had lost.

And there were other martyrs, whose names are now forgotten, who also had no share of responsibility for rebellion, who completed his work. They were those who, "crowded into the bishops' prisons, experienced," in the words of Froude,

> such miseries as the very dogs could scarcely suffer and survive. They were beaten, they were starved, they were flung into dark, fetid dens, where rotting straw was their bed, their feet were fettered in the stocks, and their clothes were their only covering, while the wretches who died in their misery were flung out into the fields where none might bury them.[13]

It was precisely because they had been guilty of no violence that these martyrs triumphed. Their sufferings sent a wave of indignation through England. A letter addressed to Bishop Bonner by a woman put the truth in a nutshell: "As for the obtaining your popish purpose in suppressing of the truth, I put you out of doubt, you shall not obtain it so long as you go this way to work as you do. You have lost the hearts of twenty thousand that were rank Papists within this twelve months."[14]

11. John Stuart Mill, *On Liberty* (London: John W. Parker & Son, 1859) 53.

12. Hugh Latimer (1487–1555) and Nicholas Ridley (1500–1555) along with Thomas Cranmer (1489–1556) are known as the Oxford Martyrs. Reformers instrumental in founding the Church of England, they were executed under Catholic Queen Mary, Henry VIII's daughter. Latimer's words to Ridley were uttered as the two men were being burned at the stake.

13. James Anthony Froude, *History of England*, vol. 5, *From the Fall of Wosley to the Defeat of the Spanish Armada* (London: Longmans, Green, 1881) 559.

14. Ibid., 561. Edmund Bonner (1500–1569) Catholic bishop of London who

Inquest on John Brown's Body

There is indeed profound truth in the saying: "The blood of the martyrs is the seed of the Church." But the blood of soldiers breeds only armed men. It was the fires of Smithfield, not war, that made England Protestant.[15]

The historian can point to a still stranger story—the story of a nation who have been Pacifists for eighteen hundred years. Originally a warlike people, war scattered them over the face of the earth. But since then, though they have been victims of innumerable persecutions, though they have been tortured and massacred, they have maintained their nationhood and their distinctive faith, without ever striking a blow in their own defense. The history of the Jews is the supreme epic of non-resistance; their survival the complete and conclusive proof of the futility of force.

But even if it were otherwise, if noble ends could be served by violence, if out of the evil of war there could be shown to come forth good, I should still say that war is wrong.

There is a simple test. To thousands of people throughout the world today Hitler is the embodiment of all that they most hate and abominate. To others, Stalin is a veritable Antichrist. Remove Hitler—or Stalin—they will sometimes tell you, and in a relatively short time Germany—or Russia—would be free and her people happy.

Suppose that you shared their belief—either of these beliefs. Suppose also that, by simply pressing a button, it was in your power to remove, to kill the man whose principles and actions filled you with so much abhorrence. Would you press the button?

It is Balzac's case of the Mandarin over again—but with this difference.[16] You are killing not to serve a personal interest, not to gain power or riches, but to rid the world of one whom you consider a menace to humanity. You may even persuade yourself that, by pressing the button, you would be performing a duty.

But would you press the button? In cold blood, could you bring yourself to do it? Would you not rather recoil in horror from the sin of murder—for

---

renounced the Protestantism he had helped institute under Henry VIII. He died in prison during Elizabeth I's reign.

15. As part of her campaign to restore Roman Catholicism to England, Queen Mary I (1516–1558) burned nearly 300 Protestants in Smithfield, a traditional place of execution in London.

16. A reference to Honore de Balzac's 1835 novel *Old Goriot*, where a character raises the possibility of making his fortune "by killing an old mandarin somewhere in China by mere force of wishing it, and without stirring from Paris" (Honore de Balzac, *Old Goriot*, trans. Ellen Marriage (London: J. M. Dent, 1913) 148).

though, slaying in this particular way, you need fear no policeman and no court of law, it would be murder just the same. And nothing, you will tell me, can justify murder.

War is only murder on a larger scale, and I refuse to believe that the killing of millions can ever be more justifiable than the killing of one.

And even if we assert, with the Jesuits, that the end justifies the means, how can we be sure, as we embark upon a "righteous" war, that its end will be righteousness? We are only men—we have no Divine foreknowledge. What we do know, if we are honest with ourselves, is that it is impossible to use the Devil's tools without doing the Devil's work.

"Thou shalt not kill" is God's commandment to mankind. Will He accept the excuse that, when we killed, we did it in His name, that we were going about His business? It seems to me that, if we make that excuse, we merely add blasphemy to murder.

V

Romance of War

A YOUNG WOMAN WAS talking to me about my Peace Movement the other day.

"And do you really want to abolish war?" she asked.

"I do," was my emphatic reply.

"But don't you think it would be rather a pity?" she objected. "You know, peace is rather dull, isn't it? And war is so romantic!"

Quite a number of young people hold that opinion. And the youth of today are the masters of tomorrow. They hold the future in their hands.

What do these young people mean when they talk about war being romantic?

They are thinking of a whole body of literature and legend which is part of the rich cultural inheritance of the race, and which glorifies the "manly" virtues and thrills us with tales of "triumph and disaster." They are thinking of marching regiments and military bands, and how their shoulders square themselves and their step quickens and keeps time to the music, and the blood seems to flow more swiftly through their veins and they feel that it is good to be alive. They are thinking of faded, tattered Colors that hang on a Cathedral wall, but once were borne into battle and which brave men guarded with their lives. They are thinking of deeds of daring and devotion, of Victoria Crosses and the cheering crowds that line the streets when the soldiers come home.

It's rather a curious complex of ideas and emotions, you see, and some of them are rather contradictory.

For instance, youth never consciously associates the romance of war with defeat, but always with victory. But the things which thrill most surely in the literature of war, in the pages of history, are the disasters rather than the triumphs. It is in the tragedy of war that we find its romance.

Perhaps, too, it is an idealized tragedy. We think of the soldier who falls, with all his wounds in front, rather than of his comrade in arms who dies of dysentery. We see those "battles long ago" through a twilight haze that softens all their harshness and gives them the quality of a dream. When we read of them, it is as if someone were telling a fairy tale, or we were seeing a play upon the stage.

Our imagination may, indeed, identify itself with certain characters; we feel certain emotions. But our selective faculty is at work all the time. We thrill to the heroic gesture, but scarcely permit ourselves to glimpse the grim despair, the agonizing pain that it concealed. Or we see these things, but see them sentimentally, like women who go to the pictures to weep over Hollywood mothers. "Oh, I did enjoy myself," they will say. "I never wept so much in my life!"

Yet it is something fine and generous in youth which responds to the old romance. I do not want to undervalue or to sneer at it. But when we come to examine, to analyze it, what do we find?

The most uniformly successful of all conquerors was Alexander the Great. But who among us remembers the name of one of Alexander's victories? The one battle of all the innumerable battles of the ancient world that we do remember—that every schoolboy has thrilled at—was of no military value whatever. After Thermopylae, the Persians had a clear road into Attica, and took it. Leonidas and his gallant handful died in vain. No second line of defense was forming behind them. Their devotion had no effect upon the final issue of the campaign.

Out of a host of men whose names made the nations terrible in those far-off days we remember Hannibal and Julius Caesar. But it is not because Hannibal won battles that he lives in history, but because his victories were fruitless. He was the leader of a forlorn hope, the champion of a lost cause. And when at last, alone and in exile, he took poison to avoid falling into the hands of the Romans, he knew that all his effort and all his genius had been wasted. The greatest master of war of classical times had accomplished exactly nothing.

And why do we still pay homage to Caesar? Why is his the greatest of all the Roman names? Not because of what he achieved—but because he

Romance of War

was struck down with his dreams still unfulfilled, his work unfinished. The daggers of his assassins gave him immortality.

At the dawn of the Middle Ages, the golden centuries of romance, we encounter Charlemagne. But we do not think of his victories, or of the Empire which he built—our minds leap to the Song of Roland and the hero who died in the Pass of Roncesvalles.

All though history, romance goes hand in hand with defeat, frustration, death. Elizabeth of England was a great Queen, and her policies were crowned with success, but it is Mary of Scots who still has power to wring our hearts and bring the moisture to our eyes.

Montrose on the scaffold, the Jacobite exiles eating out their hearts in exile, far from the scenes and sounds of home, Bonnie Prince Charlie flying from his enemies, with a price on his head—here is romance. And would Napoleon appeal so much to the imagination if there had been no retreat from Moscow, no Elba, no Waterloo, no St. Helena?

But what, looking back, we see as romance, was once reality. The actors in these dramas found them desperately earnest. Do you think that Mary of Scots visualized herself as a romantic legend during those nineteen years she spent in English prisons? Or as she dressed and arranged her hair for the last time that grim morning at Fotheringay?

Remember, too, the multitudes who died that Napoleon might bestride Europe like a Colossus and make his marshals kings. We see him as a heroic figure, but how many mothers cursed him? The ghosts that thronged the death chamber at St. Helena were not the ghosts of old romance, but the great company of those who died because of one man's dream of world dominion.

I also have felt the magic of resounding names, have thrilled to the stories of great deeds. But always a shadow falls across the printed page and I think of homes made desolate and young lives spilt and wasted and women who mourned "the unreturning brave."

Now the young people who think that war is romantic know that war means death, that wherever the nations are joined in conflict men and women are killed. But they only know it vaguely—they don't realize what it means. Very few of them have ever seen a man die. They've certainly never seen a battlefield.

They are prepared to go to war in exactly the same careless spirit as they go out for a weekend run in a sports car. When they do that they don't think of the road casualty figures. But I've known cases where youthful speed-merchants, going out intent on seeing how quickly they could get from one place to another, have returned home, traveling very discreetly and looking very subdued. They have witnessed an accident, they have seen maimed and broken bodies being lifted from out the wreckage of a road smash.

A very little experience of war would quickly produce a similar revulsion of feeling. I believe that this is true of any sort of war. It is only at a distance, or in retrospect, that war has ever been romantic. At close quarters it has always been a nightmare of blood and pain and boredom, dirt and vermin and disease.

But let us assume, for a moment, that there have been wars which were true to the romantic pattern, in which youth could realize all its heroic dreams. War is certainly not like that today. We turn from our contemplation of the old romance to look at the new reality. As Mr. Winston Churchill writes in *My Early Life*,

> War, which used to be cruel and magnificent, has now become cruel and squalid. In fact it has been completely spoilt. It is all the fault of Democracy and Science. From the moment that either of these meddlers and muddlers was allowed to take part in actual fighting, the doom of War was sealed. Instead of a small number of well-trained professionals championing their country's cause with ancient weapons and a beautiful intricacy of archaic maneuver, sustained at every moment by the applause of their nation, we now have entire populations, including even women and children, pitted against one another in brutish mutual extermination, and only a set of blear-eyed clerks left to add up the butcher's bill. From the moment Democracy was admitted to, or rather forced itself upon the battlefield, War ceased to be a gentleman's game. To Hell with it![1]

That is rather a remarkable passage. You will find in it an appreciation of all that youth comprehends in the term "the romance of war" and a regretful admission that it no longer exists.

I call another witness, the late Field Marshal Sir William Robertson. His view was substantially the same. "War was all right fifty years ago. It's a fool's game now. Fifty years ago it was fought in a more or less just and sportsmanlike manner. With the thousand and one mechanical barbarities attached to it today, it is merely a horror."[2]

---

1. Winston Churchill, *My Early Life: A Roving Commission* (New York: Scribner's, 1958) 65.

2. Sir William Robert Robertson (1860–1933) Chief of the Imperial General Staff for the final two years of World War I. Robertson is the only British soldier to rise in rank from private to field marshal.

Romance of War

If youth wants more detail before relinquishing the dream of romantic war, Marshal Foch has supplied it:

> The next war will be a world war in the fullest sense of the word, and, moreover, it can no longer be isolated. Almost all countries will take part in it, and not only the men but the women and children will fight too. Poison gas bombs will spread deadly fumes which will penetrate any mask and produce death in a few minutes. Phosphorus bombs, impossible to extinguish, will burn the flesh to the bone within half a minute.
>
> Hundreds of tanks, each one able to shoot a thousand deadly bullets a minute, machine guns like automatic rifles which, in the hands of 1,000,000 men, will shoot 100,000,000 bullets a minute, will also be raging, and the heavens above will be darkened by a thousand aeroplanes pouring a rain of horror on the earth. Behind the lines, cities and villages will crumble in ruins under the destructive fire of the latest artillery. In the next war there will be no such thing as the front and the rear. The whole nation will find itself on the firing line.[3]

None of these descriptions of modern war is the work of a Pacifist, trying to frighten people into renouncing the use of arms. But in case you think that soldiers are sometimes scaremongers and that these warnings may be exaggerated, let us see what some civilians who have studied the matter have to say. Mr. J. L. Garvin wrote in 1925,

> Let us shake ourselves out of a dream and try to visualize the real character of a next war. The speed and efficiency of air squadrons is continually increasing. They will strike at the heart. Their bombs will crash continually on the dense cities without respect to age or sex. Poison fumes will choke and kill. Fire will ravage. The shattering, the stifling, the conflagrations will go on together. The civilian population will have the weight of casualties, not the armies and navies. Over the heads of the armies and navies invasion will occur in its most intense and devastating form . . .
>
> By the last paradox of modern war, it would be safer to be a soldier than a civilian in a large town.[4]

Here is a strange new sidelight on the "romance of war." To youth the idea of romance implies danger and the willing acceptance of danger. But

---

3. Ferdinand Foch (1851–1929) Marshal of France who was appointed Generalissimo of the Allied Armies toward the end of World War I.

4. James Lewis Garvin (1868–1947) editor of the British weekly *The Observer* for over thirty years.

this forecast suggests that those who join the armed forces may be accepting danger for others rather than for themselves, that enlistment may be a sort of running away and leaving mothers and wives and children in the post of peril.

The phrase "women and children first" thus acquires a new significance. "There is a mustard gas," says Emil Ludwig, "that will stick to a person's shoes and be carried inside houses, where it will burn first of all the tender skins of little children." He adds: "Whereas thirty different kinds of poison gases had been developed in 1914, today [1931] there are more than 1,000 different kinds which with refined mixtures or sequences will be able to attack and destroy one by one the human organs. The sufferings of the martyrs of the future will be beyond anything endured by the medieval martyrs who were burned at the stake or tortured on the rack."[5]

But, it may be objected, war is subject to rules, and weapons of the kind which I am describing will not be permitted. In the article I have already quoted, Mr. Garvin says:

> The idea of war on limited liability is the most pathetic of human delusions. If you are to have it at all you must have it at its worst, and cannot have it otherwise . . . As the machines, the forces, the agents, the brains of the scientific age become more terrible in perversion, what we call armed conflict, if resumed by an ill-fated world, must become more relentless, unsparing, until civilization perishes from a misuse of the powers that might have raised modern life to a new grandeur and happiness and beauty . . .
>
> Unless we abolish war itself, by no means on earth can we lessen its instruments or mitigate its horrors . . . Its means necessarily include every device which can inflict slaughter, mutilation, torture and destruction . . . War is as bad now as once when cannibalism was the end of it, or when hands and feet were cut off and eyes put out and babies spitted.

Still we have not exhausted the possibilities of modern warfare. Professor Leonard Hill, a year or two ago, described a bacillus which, he said according to *The London Times* report of his speech, was easily cultivated.

> If men were as susceptible as guinea pigs were to the toxin produced by this bacillus—and there are reason to think that they are—it would appear that one gramme, say a saltspoonful, of the toxin would suffice to kill a million. The toxin acted if inhaled or if it fell on the eye as a powder. If men set out to prepare such a

5. Emil Ludwig (1881–1948) German author and biographer.

toxin and scatter it by aeroplane, what would be the use of the panoply of war?⁶

It is true that to disseminate disease as an act of war is to employ a two-edged weapon. Frontiers have never yet succeeded in stopping the march of an epidemic, and the nation which calls pestilence to its aid may itself be overwhelmed by the dark forces it has released. But those who wage war are notoriously short-sighted.

I have quoted a number of statements made by experts over a period of years. I think it may be taken for granted that research has not been standing still in the meantime, and that the dangers which threaten the world today are greater rather than less. But there is a tendency to minimize them, to insist that the potentialities, for instance, of aerial bombing have been exaggerated, and to suggest that means of defense against it may be found.

This change of tone is not reassuring. Men can afford to face squarely those evils which they believe are remote. As they approach more nearly, are felt to be inevitable, a protective psychology asserts itself, and there is a tendency to pretend that perhaps the things we fear are not quite so bad after all.

Even now, however, there are still realists who refuse to deceive either themselves or others. On the same day that Mr. Ramsay MacDonald spoke hopefully in the House of Commons about "a promising line of research" which might afford protection against bombing, Mr. Winston Churchill told the same assembly that the only effective means of defense was retaliation.⁷

Mr. Churchill's speech was a plea for a bigger Air Force. I disagree with his demand absolutely, but, if his premises are accepted, the logic of his position is unassailable. If we are to fight, we will use the weapons that our enemies use, and we will use them in exactly the same way. If they bomb our cities, and kill our women and children, we will bomb their cities, and kill their women and children. And if we believe that this may happen, and that it is justifiable, then we must be at least as strong and as well prepared for war as our prospective antagonists.

At least we know where we are with Mr. Churchill. But what are we to make of Mr. Baldwin? Speaking four days later, he said: "I wish, for many reasons, that flying had never been invented. But it has been. Men never go back on their inventions, and somehow we have got to Christianize it."⁸

6. Sir Leonard Erskin Hill (1866–1952) British physiologist.

7. Throughout the mid- and late-1930s, Churchill, alarmed at the rise of German fascism, was a continuous advocate of enlarging and modernizing the Royal Air Force.

8. Stanley Baldwin (1867–1947) Conservative Prime Minister on three different

If this means anything at all, it means that Mr. Baldwin is still hankering after some means by which the nations can contract out of the horrors of aerial warfare while force still remains the final arbiter in international disputes. It is the pathetic delusion of "war on limited liability" which Mr. Garvin dismissed so contemptuously. And if Mr. Baldwin becomes once again a Minister in a War Government he will be forced to abandon these ideas of his and adopt Mr. Churchill's.

We have to face the fact that, so long as we accept war as a possibility, there is no weapon which we can rule out. Indeed, how are we, in fairness, to ask men to join the armed forces in order to defend us and then deny them the use of the latest and most efficient weapons? During the first phase of the Great War thousands of our troops lost their lives because of the fact that our artillery was firing shrapnel instead of high explosive shells.

But, of course, in a new war, our soldiers and sailors and airmen will not be able to defend, but only to avenge us.

I do not wish, however, to labor this point. It has not been my purpose, in this chapter, to try to frighten people into accepting my point of view. I do not believe that we will ever abolish war because we are afraid of its consequences. But I want to give those young people who still cling to the fantasy that war is romantic some idea of what it really involves. And I want to ask them a question.

I want to ask them, not: "Are you prepared to suffer all this?" but something which is much more serious and much more fundamental: Are you prepared to inflict all this? Are you prepared, from the comparative safety of a seat in an aeroplane, to shower down on a defenseless city those gases that will burn the skin and eat into the lungs of women and little children? Are you prepared to be part of the organization behind this grim rain of torture and pestilence and death?

This is the work to which the next war will call the youth of our own and every other belligerent nation. Those engaged in it will have, of course, the consolation—and the excuse—that their own mothers and sisters and wives and babies are being served in exactly the same way by the enemy. They will also be risking their own lives.

But I do not think they will persuade themselves very easily that they are heroes, or that there is much of romance in their activities. And I do not know how they will make their peace with God.

---

occasions in the 1920s and 1930s, made this remark after reading a secret intelligence report about the destruction that German warplanes could inflict on British cities.

VI

The Slayer of Souls

―――――

When we talk of the evil of war, what we usually have in mind is its waste of life. We point to the Great War cemeteries, with their rows upon rows of little crosses, that bear mute witness to lives cut short and homes plunged into mourning. We point to the great company of maimed and broken men, to twisted bodies, and eyes that shall never again see the burgeoning of spring or the glory of summer, or look upon the cornfields at harvest; and faces that are ghastly masks of horror.

But war does not only destroy men's bodies. It destroys their souls as well. And that, I think, is more terrible than anything it does to the physical part of us.

To my mind, one of the grimmest of all the stories of the war is that of the British soldier who suffered from the extraordinary "delusion," every time that he saw a German, that here was a man who probably had a wife and children, a mother and sisters and brothers, just like himself. The practical results of this strange fantasy were not conducive to military efficiency.

So the man was sent away for treatment by the Army psychologists. *They cured him.*

That story is one of the most damning indictments of war it is possible to conceive. It shows how war remakes men's minds in its own image—how it destroys or represses every instinct, every impulse, every thought, every feeling that might interfere with the smooth working of the machinery of slaughter.

For you must not think that this is an isolated case. The only remarkable thing about it is that the psychologists had to be called in and the man had to be treated as an individual. So far as the great mass of the population was concerned, the same results were obtained, almost from the moment of the ultimatum, by means of large-scale war propaganda.

It is easy to laugh at propaganda and to say that no sensible person is affected by it. The majority of people still believe what they are told, and ideas which are widely held and colored by strong emotion create an atmosphere from which it is difficult to escape. Even a wise man may act foolishly when he finds himself one of a mob. He looks back on his conduct with horror and disgust once he is safely home again, but for the time being, unless he possesses exceptional will power, he is swept off his feet. Reason abdicates, and he becomes only a channel, one of the many channels, through which the mob expresses itself and realizes its purpose. In war we are all caught in a mob.

This fact has been very clearly recognized in the United States. One of the declarations they are inviting the young men of America to sign begins:

> I have quietly considered what I would do if my nation should again be drawn into war. I am not taking a pledge, because I do not know what I would do when the heat of the war mood is upon the country. But in a mood of calm consideration I do today declare that I cannot reconcile the way of Christ with the practice of war.[1]

Dr. Henry H. Crane expresses the same fear of the power of propaganda and the mob emotion it arouses in a still more forcible way.

> So help me God, I will never bless, sanction, nor participate in another war! How do I know? I don't. I simply assert the deepest conviction of my being—while I am still sane, emotionally stable and utterly sincere. Should another war come, I might go. I'm all too fallible, weak and capable of cowardice. That's why I want to go on record *now*. So that, should I go, no one shall salute me, eulogize me, nor attempt to glorify me. Rather, they must hiss, revile and condemn me for what I should be revealing myself to be: a moral coward, a propagandized puppet, a mob-minded murderer, a world traitor, a Christ crucifier.[2]

---

1. This pledge was written in 1940 by the New York Broadway Tabernacle, an Assemblies of God congregation, and recommended to other congregations. At the time, the Assemblies of God was pacifist. But after Pearl Harbor, it abandoned its endorsement of nonviolence to support the war effort.

2. Crane was an American clergyman long involved in anti-war activity. In 1944, he

As these American Churchmen have learned by bitter experience, hysteria always involves a weakening of moral fiber, and the mass hysteria of wartime is perhaps the most powerful of all the destroyers of decency and courage. It is rather like trying to stand up to an avalanche to oppose it, but because the soul is stronger than the body there are people who are able to do it.

In the Army, for those who join up, there is added to this powerful mass suggestion an intensive training in hatred and brutality. It is not always completely effective; on the whole, during the last war, the old men who stayed at home—and a good many of the women—were more bloodthirsty than the majority of the soldiers. But it is usually effective up to a point.

I am not concerned for the moment with any question of blame. If war is necessary, then men must be made fit to wage it—in other words, they must be brutalized. Machiavelli saw that over 400 years ago, when he wrote in *The Prince*: "There are two methods of fighting, the one by law, the other by force: the first method is that of men, the second of beasts . . . It is therefore necessary to know well how to use both the beast and the man."[3] The world has repudiated the teacher, but it has learned the lesson. Before you protest, read Brigadier-General F. P. Crozier's remarkable war book, *A Brass Hat in No Man's Land*.[4] Describing the psychological side of the training of young soldiers during the war, he says:

> The British soldier is a kindly fellow, and it is safe to say, despite the dope, seldom oversteps the mark of barbaric propriety in France . . .
>
> In order that he shall enter into the true spirit of the show, however, the fun of the fair as we may call it, it is necessary to corrode his mentality with bittersweet vice and to keep him up to the vicious scratch on all occasions. Casualties are never alluded to save in the vein of callous or careless regret . . . By September, 1915, everything we do is faultless, everything the Germans do is abominable. It is the only way in war, and both sides follow it.

was one of the American endorsers of Vera Brittain's "Massacre by Bombing," an indictment of Allied saturation bombing of Germany.

3. The quote is from chapter 18 of *The Prince*.

4. Crozier (1879–1937) was a highly decorated frontline general in World War I whose 1931 anti-war memoir *A Brass Hat in No Man's Land* frankly described typically unpublicized aspects of war such as the execution of sentries caught sleeping on duty or the shooting of prisoners of war. In the 1920s, Crozier joined the League of Nations Union and, afterwards, Sheppard's Peace Pledge Union. The publication of his memoir scandalized his old comrades in arms.

> I regard this course of suggestion as a means to an end. I can adopt the pose at will. I do not really hate the Germans—I say I do. I really do not like to "see the red blood flow," but there are men who will swear to this day that I like nothing better . . .[5]

So much for the training. General Crozier also describes its results. Here is a cameo of wartime chivalry:

> The enemy fall like grass before the scythe. "Damned_____," shouts an officer, "give them hell." I look through my glasses.
> "Good heavens," I shout, "these men are prisoners surrendering, and some of our own wounded are escorting them. Cease fire, cease fire, for God's sake!" The fire ripples on for a time. The target is too good to lose. "After all they are only Germans," I hear a youngster say.[6]

General Crozier also tells a story of how a bullying N.C.O. in a British regiment was murdered by the men whose lives he had made unbearable. A live bomb was placed between his back and his trousers and blew him to bits.

By the time that he wrote his book, General Crozier had become convinced of the futility of war as a method of settling disputes between nations, but I do not think that this fact has led him to exaggerate. I know that the men of the New Armies were trained in brutality. I know it because I have seen it with my own eyes and heard it with my own ears. I have watched while a bayonet instructor described and demonstrated the techniques of fighting at close quarters to a squad of young soldiers.

There is, indeed, plenty of evidence of deliberate brutalization. Mr. Stephen Graham,[7] in his book, *A Private in the Guards*, gives a vivid picture of how "civvies" were knocked into shape by drill sergeants whose aim was "not only to train the muscles but to break or bend the intelligence." He says:

---

5. Crozier, *A Brass Hat in No Man's Land* (London: Jonathan Cape, 1930) 43–44. Curiously, Sheppard chose to omit the ending of the first full sentence he quoted. Crozier wrote that the British soldier "seldom oversteps the mark of barbaric propriety in France, *save occasionally to kill prisoners he cannot be bothered to escort back to his lines*."

6. Ibid., 108.

7. Journalist and author Graham (1884–1975) spent the first years of World War I in Russia as a war correspondent. Returning to Britain, he enlisted in the Scots Guards and saw frontline service toward the end of the war. His memoir *A Private in the Guards* (1919) offers a shocking portrayal of the harshness of military training and discipline.

Constant humiliation and the use of indecent phrases took down the recruit's pride, and reduced him to a condition when he was amenable to any command. It is impossible not to think less of yourself when a sergeant has bawled before a whole squad: "Well, I think you're about the ugliest thing ever dropped from a woman"; or, "Are you married? Fancy a decent woman having children by a man like you."

To be struck, to be threatened, to be called indecent names, to be drilled by yourself in front of a squad in order to make a fool of you, to be commanded to do a tiring exercise and continue doing it whilst the rest of the squad does something else; to have your ear spat into, to be marched across parade ground under escort, to be falsely accused before an officer and silenced when you try to speak in defense—all these things take down your pride, make you feel small and in some ways fit you to accept the role of cannon fodder on the battleground.[8]

Yet, at least in part, this is "the only discipline fitting for the new stress of war." "In wartime," says Mr. Graham, "the problem of breaking in those who were never intended by Nature to be soldiers was so difficult that some of these ugly things become useful."[9]

Men who go through such a training can never be quite the same again. But, to be fair, I do not think that those methods were universal. They were not employed by the Australians, and I believe that there were a number of British regiments which did not find them necessary. The difference, however, was perhaps one of degree rather than kind. Brutalization, to a greater or less extent, was an inevitable result of all military training.

And for all who were ready in time, after the barracks square came the battlefield. What does it mean to kill a man? Can you realize what it means to slay and experience a sense of exhilaration in the act?

That is one of the most fantastically terrible things about war—it releases impulses and appetites and lusts that men never dreamed they possessed. As Mr. Henry de Man—incidentally, before the war an International Socialist and Peace propagandist—has confessed in *The Re-Making of a Mind*, there is a "joy of killing."[10]

8. Graham, *A Private in the Guards* (London: Macmillan, 1919) 58.

9. Ibid.

10. Henri de Man, *The Re-Making of a Mind: A Soldier's Thoughts on War and Reconstruction* (New York: Scribner's, 1919) 197. De Man's book is a study, based on his experiences in the Belgian army during World War I, of the psychological effects of battle on soldiers.

Mr. de Man believes that this "joy of killing" is part of the make-up of most men, or might become so. But, though he has felt it himself, he does not consider it a virtue. He also utters a warning which the Governments of the world would do well to ponder when they contemplate another war:

> Should conditions arise in the life of these masses that either make it in their interest to murder, or else create a common feeling in favor of class terrorism, they might remember how easy it is to take another man's life, and what a delight there is in doing it.[11]

You may say that it is only exceptional men, here and there, who experience this "joy of killing"—that for the average soldier it is a regrettable necessity. I am afraid it is the other way round, and that Mr. de Man is right. I have talked to many soldiers, and not a few of them have been frank with me. I remember, too, the satisfaction of certain civilians as they read of "enemy losses" in their newspapers, their delight in vicarious slaughter. Dr. Harry Emerson Fosdick has painted a vivid word picture of that aspect of war. "I hate war for what it forces us to do to our enemies," he has written, "slaying their children with our blockades, bombing their mothers in their villages, and laughing at our breakfast tables over our coffee cups at every damnable and devilish thing we have been able to do to them."[12]

You also, if you recall the war days, may remember experiencing a similar hellish mirth.

And it was not only vicarious satisfactions that some of our civilians enjoyed. Their bloodlust occasionally found direct expression. Do you recollect what happened to some of those who had German names, or were suspected of being spies and of signaling to the enemy? No picture of what war does to the souls of men and women would be complete without some description of this. Here is a cameo from *The Home Front*, by Sylvia Pankhurst:

> A crowd was advancing at a run, a couple of lads on bicycles leading, a swarm of children on the fringes, screaming like gulls. Missiles were flying. In the center of the turmoil men dragged a big, stout man, stumbling and resisting in their grasp . . . his mouth dripping blood. They rushed him on. New throngs closed round him . . . From another direction arose more shouting. A

---

11. Ibid., 200.

12. Harry Emerson Fosdick, "A Christian Conscience about War," a sermon delivered at the League of Nations assembly service in Geneva, Switzerland, 13 September 1925. Fosdick (1878–1969) American Protestant pastor, was a leader in the anti-fundamentalist and Christian pacifist movements in the United States.

woman's scream. The tail of the crowd dashed off towards the sound. Crowds raced to it from all directions . . . fierce, angry shouts and yells. . . . A woman was in the midst of a struggling mob; her blouse half torn off, her fair hair fallen, her face contorted with pain and terror, blood running down her bare white arm. A big, drunken man flung her to the ground. She was lost to sight . . . "Oh, my God! Oh! They are kicking her!" a woman screamed.[13]

You see to what a level war reduces us. Take another picture, this time of what happened to conscientious objectors in the United States. It consists of extracts from a daily record quoted by Norman Thomas in *The Conscientious Objector in America*:

> He (the officer of the day) then had our beds and blankets taken from us, and ordered that we be given raw rations—pork and beans—which we were to cook in the latrine, if we wanted to eat. He suggested to the prisoners that they beat us up . . .
> At 8 p.m. the "officer of the day," a captain, and the sergeant of the guard ordered all to undress in the squadron and prepare for a cold shower, the third that day. We were marched to the latrine in a body. The Captain himself brought forth scrub brushes, used ordinarily for cleaning toilet seats, and brooms used for sweeping, and ordered that we scrub each other with them. Franklin refused to use the filthy brush. He was seized and roughly thrown to the cement floor, dragged back and forth and viciously belabored until thoroughly exhausted. He was then placed under the cold spray and left there until he collapsed. Eichel and Shotkin helped him back to his bed. When he recovered he became hysterical.[14]

America, of course, is a new country, and almost its only tradition is one of violence and brutality in its dealings with those on the wrong side of the law or of public opinion. But were we in Britain very much better? In his book, *Conscription and Conscience—A History, 1916-1919*, John W. Graham quotes an account by Garth Ballantyne of a military prison camp near Dunkirk, "not because its hardships specially fell upon conscientious objectors, but because they were, on the contrary, the doom of ordinary

---

13. Sylvia Pankhurst, *The Home Front* (London: Hutchinson, 1930) 194. Pankhurst (1882-1960) was an outspoken suffragette and opponent of World War I.

14. Norman Thomas, *The Conscientious Objector in America* (New York: Huebsch, 1923) 160. Thomas (1884-1958) was a Presbyterian minister, socialist, and pacifist who ran for the U.S. presidency six times.

soldiers." "The inmates," says Mr. Graham, "were not criminals, but had broken discipline in some form."¹⁵

Ballantyne, after a bullying reception intended to cow him, refused to obey an order, and was punished by "solitary confinement, with bread and water, wearing figure of eight handcuffs for about twelve hours a day." His food was "eight ounces of dry bread at seven in the morning, with water, and the same at five in the evening." He says:

> Generally, when a prisoner was sent to the cells for punishment he was first taken into a cell, stripped naked, sometimes handcuffed; then the warder would proceed to administer a sound thrashing, using both his hands and feet, one warder, during his turn in charge of the cells, going so far as to use a heavy leather belt. Then, when the prisoner was beginning to get groggy, buckets of freezing cold water would be thrown over him to revive him, and finally he would be given a bucket and cloth and be told to dry up his cell before he would be given back his clothes. Often the bumps and thuds of the poor prisoner against the iron walls and his yells and cries for mercy could be heard all over the compound.¹⁶

Re-read that last paragraph, and then remind yourself that it isn't a description of what happens in a German concentration camp, but of a British military prison in wartime, and that among those subject to this discipline there were doubtless boys who had joined the Army as volunteers, in order to "make the world safe for democracy."

Do I need to adduce further evidence of the brutalizing effects of war? Do I need to describe, for instance, Field Punishment No. 1: a form of crucifixion, but without the nails?¹⁷

There are, however, two more aspects of the power of war over the souls of men to which I wish to refer. There are many men in mental institutions today because their minds gave way under the stress of battle. There are innumerable others whose minds are permanently scarred as the result of war neuroses.

If war came tomorrow, there are large numbers of young men who would join up, not because they wanted to go to war, but because they were

15. John W. Graham, *Conscription and Conscience: A History, 1916–1919* (London: Allen & Unwin, 1922) 129.

16. Graham, *Conscription and Conscience*, 130–31.

17. Field Punishment Number 1, used frequently by the British Army during World War I, was a form of public humiliation in which the offender was tied to a stake or sometimes a caisson wheel, usually spread-eagled, for up to two hours at a time.

afraid of being thought cowards. They ought to know that war makes cowards. There is a point at which endurance snaps, at which the mind ceases to function, and the spirit of man abdicates, leaving his body, a mass of quivering nerves, under the lash of fear.

For every one of us this breaking point exists, though it varies with different individuals. But, as between two men in whom it is approximately the same, it may be very largely a matter of luck which of them is decorated for bravery and which is shot at dawn for cowardice or desertion.

The time factor also counts for a good deal. "Any man who spent six months in the line (which almost inevitably meant taking part in a big battle) and then claimed that he had never felt fear, never received any shock to his nerves, never had his heart thumping and his throat dry with apprehension, was either superhuman, subnormal, or a liar," says Richard Aldington in *Death of a Hero*.

> The newest troops were nearly always the least affected. They were not braver, they were merely fresher. There were very few—were there any? —who could resist week after week, month after month of the physical or mental strain. It is absurd to talk about men being brave or cowards. There were greater or less degrees of sensibility, more or less self-control. The longer the strain on the finer sensibility, the greater the self-control needed. But this continual neurosis steadily became worse and required a greater effort of repression.[18]

Now have a look at what may happen when at last breaking-point is reached. Here is a case of shell shock, as described by Arthur Osburn in *Unwilling Passenger*:

> The Staff Officer, a biggish man, somewhere between twenty-five and thirty, lay moaning on the ground. We could find no wound. In the din I tried to question him, thinking he had been seized with a fit or with acute internal pain. But he only moaned and jabbered and shook his head groveling on the ground at my feet with his face pressed to the muddy floor. While I questioned him we were suddenly assailed by a more than usually heavy burst of shelling ...

---

18. Richard Aldington, *Death of a Hero* (London: Chatto & Windus, 1929) 332. Aldington (1892–1962) joined the British Army in 1916 and was wounded on the Western Front the following year. He subsequently suffered from what today would be diagnosed as post traumatic stress disorder. *Death of a Hero* is a fictionalized account of his war experiences.

> The groveling object appeared now to be suddenly seized with a fresh access of terror. Wildly and incoherently he made efforts to conceal himself between the remains of a broken chair and the mud wall of the shelter. Then suddenly, spasmodically, he began to dig furiously with his fingers . . . Driven mad with terror, slobbering and moaning, he clawed and scrabbled violently in the mud, his head under the chair . . . Extreme terror had driven him back through a thousand generations to some pre-human form of life.[19]

Arthur Osburn goes on to contrast the fate of that Staff Officer with that of "some poor, half-educated, blubbering ploughboy, whose nerves had likewise given way . . . sent back to face the enemy or be shot for cowardice."[20]

You think you would stand up to things better? You might. But none of us knows his own weakness, and, terrible as shellfire was in the last war, it will be still more terrible in the next.

If a young man is afraid of being, or being thought, a coward, his mother has another fear—that he will suffer moral contamination. She is thinking of morality in its narrower, rather than its wider sense, but her dread is most certainly justified. Brigadier General Crozier, whom I have already quoted, is as frank on this as on other matters. "It is not reasonable," he says, "to expect the youngsters to keep the trenches for England intact and their chastity inviolable at one and the same time. He who hopes to wage war without wine and women is living in a fool's paradise, for there are no half measures in war, try how one will."[21]

This was generally recognized by the authorities during the Great War. There is an ironical contrast between Lord Kitchener's message to the soldier going on active service: "Your duty cannot be done unless your health is sound, so be constantly on your guard against any excesses. In this new experience you may find temptations, both in wine and women. You must entirely resist both temptations, and, while treating all women with perfect courtesy, you should avoid any intimacy," and the spectacle that soldier found awaiting him overseas, of long queues of Tommies in the street outside the brothels of the towns behind the lines.[22]

---

19. Arthur Osburn, *Unwilling Passenger* (London: Faber & Faber, 1932) 291. Osburn (1876–1952) served in the RAMC (Royal Army Medical Corps) both before and during World War I.

20. Ibid., 292.

21. Crozier, *A Brass Hat in No Man's Land*, 127.

22. This bit of advice, issued at the beginning of the war to each British soldier, was

No doubt many young soldiers were kept away from the red lamps by an innate fastidiousness, but many more went, if only from curiosity. Some of these carried away with them, from that first visit, the seeds of abominable disease; others, more fortunate, escaped with nothing worse than self-loathing and a sense of ineffaceable shame. They had spoilt and degraded what should have been sacred. Their feelings have been expressed by a soldier who served on the Salonica Front:[23]

> This is not Love? The gesture is the same;
> The highest passion seeks but this same end.
> May I know Love hereafter? On my wedding night,
> Between my bride's pale purity and me,
> Between her pouting lips and mine that search
> To wake her sleeping woman's nature there,
> Shall not rise up the image of this thing,
> These cold lips tired of kisses, and that sex
> Aweary of its function?

But even those who shunned the bought kisses of the prostitute were not always proof against other forms of promiscuity. It was, indeed, only natural that, amid the hectic excitements of the war period, moral bonds should be loosened and standards of conduct relaxed. War is ever a whip to sex.

Yet some of us who were parsons were foolish enough to believe, in the early months of the fighting, that this ordeal through which the nation was passing would deepen and intensify spiritual values, and arouse us to a new apprehension of the things of God. We learned as the years passed that men who live constantly in the shadow of sudden death are more apt to turn to the Devil than to God. They grasp frantically at whatever passing pleasure is offered them, regardless of its price, because they know that tomorrow the fires of youth may be quenched forever, and desire and dream be swallowed in the grave.

---

prefaced with: "This paper is to be considered by each soldier as confidential, and to be kept in his Active Service Pay Book." Horatio Herbert Kitchener (1850–1916) decorated Field Marshall in the British Army who served during the opening years of World War I as Secretary of State for War. He perished when the warship on which he was traveling to Russia was sunk by a German mine.

23. Also known as the Macedonian Front, an unsuccessful Allied attempt in 1915 to hold back German, Austro-Hungarian, and Bulgarian military forces from overrunning Serbia.

We Say NO!

I do not pretend to blame them. This corruption of youth is one of the inevitable consequences of war. It is part of the indictment that I bring against war as a slayer of souls.

Are we again to expose our sons to all this? I think that I may almost add: Are we to expose our daughters to all this? The Rev. A. Belden, speaking at a meeting of the Women's International Peace Crusade in London in March, 1935, said:

> Don't forget that in the mad war that the next war will be, if it comes, the first incidence of mass murder will fall upon the women and children of the densely massed industrial populations, and do not let the girls forget either that it is practically certain that they will be required to pilot aeroplanes for the bombing of their sisters in other lands and cities.[24]

Fantastic? Martha Jane Graber, a nurse, born in Alsace Lorraine, applied to an American court for the rights and privileges of citizenship of the United States. She was asked if she was willing to serve the country in time of war. She replied that she would do so in keeping with the spirit of her profession—she was a nurse. That reply was not considered satisfactory.

"Suppose your country saw fit to demand your service in the army in time of war as a combatant, to take part in the war; explain what you would do under such circumstances," she was asked.

"I would go to the front in my profession," replied Miss Graber.

"That doesn't answer my question," pursued the inquisitor. "My question is: Suppose you were called upon to act as a combatant in time of war for the United States, would you fight?"

"That would not be professional as a nurse."

"That doesn't answer the question: Are you willing to fight for the United States if need be? You understand what is meant by fighting, Miss Graber; I mean to take up arms in defense of the United States if necessary."

"I cannot kill, but I would be willing to give my life."

"Do I understand that you mean that you are unwilling to fight for the United States?"

"Do you mean by 'fighting,' 'killing'?"

"I do if necessary. Such is war, Miss Graber."

"Do you want an answer or what?"

---

24. The Women's Peace Crusade was founded in 1917 largely through the efforts of Charlotte Despard (1844–1939) Irish suffragette, pacifist, and animal rights activist.

"The question is as to whether or not in time of war, if need be, you are willing to shed blood in defense of the United States?"

"I said I would be willing to shed my own blood to protect this government."

"I am not asking you as to your willingness to shed your own blood. I am asking you as to your willingness to shed the blood of others if need be."

"I conscientiously could not do that."

Miss Graber's application for citizenship was rejected.[25]

In view of this cross examination, does Mr. Belden's prophecy seem quite so absurd? Remember, too, that women, as well as men, are being trained to bear arms in Soviet Russia. If a war should break out in which that country is engaged, and if she puts women into the field as well as men, the nations on the other side must either do the same or fight at a tremendous disadvantage with regard to reserves. I do not know if there is any country in the world where the spirit of chivalry would be strong enough to withstand that test.

But I would like the old men, who were so patriotically ready to sacrifice the young men's lives in the last war, to think whether they will have no qualms in sending their daughters into battle as well. Not because they may be killed or maimed—in the next war that may happen to them just as easily at home—but because of what may be done to their minds and souls.

It is useless to say that things will never come to this. The whole tendency of today is to establish a substantial equality—of duties and responsibilities as well as of privileges—between the sexes, and physically the average girl is now as strong, as adaptable, and as capable of endurance as her brother.

There is, in fact, only one way of making sure that it will never come to this. And that is by making sure that there will be no more war.

---

25. Martha Jane Graber was a Mennonite, living and working as a nurse in Ohio, who sought U.S. citizenship prior to departing for Africa as a medical missionary. She appealed her rejection all the way to the Supreme Court, which in 1930 upheld the earlier decisions. The case, which attracted widespread attention in the U.S. and Europe, prompted congressional debate the following year about the propriety of rejecting applications for citizenship simply because the petitioner was a pacifist.

VII

If They Raped Your Sister

——— —— ———

LET US SUPPOSE THAT I have been libeling the nations of the world. Let us suppose, at least, that, whatever other countries may do, Britain will never mobilize its womanhood under the banners of battle. We will still be able to say that we are fighting for hearth and home, in defense of wives and mothers and sisters and children.

There is a certain value in this, from the militarist point of view. When the believer in force debates with the Pacifist, his final, clinching argument, after he has been worsted on every other point, always begins: "But if they raped your sister—." (Sometimes there is a variation, "But if they raped your mother—" but, on the whole, especially if the Pacifist's mother is getting on in life, a sister is a more probable victim.)

Now, I have not the slightest doubt that, if you saw someone making an attempt to rape your sister, you would do what you could to prevent it. Probably it would be rather unnecessary, as the average young woman of today is quite capable of defending her own honor against assault. However, you would go to her rescue—and you would be perfectly right to do so.

Just a minute, however. If, as the militarist supposes, the rape takes place in wartime, and if, in order to safeguard your sister's chastity, you have already joined one of the fighting services, you will probably be hundreds of miles away, and quite unable to do anything to help.

Even if you were within earshot, and could hear your sister calling for assistance, if you were under military discipline, you might not be allowed to go to her. There might be other things for you to do which, from the military point of view, were much more urgent and important.

True, the court martial which tried you, or the General who reviewed its sentence, might decide that your sister's plight was an extenuating circumstance. But if, at the time, you were in action, you might never come before a court martial. You might be shot, out of hand, by your officer. Under Army law, he would be perfectly entitled to shoot a soldier who was running away—as you would appear to be doing—in face of the enemy.

The militarist, however, does not visualize circumstances like these. What he really suggests is this—that any man with a spark of manhood in him would be prepared to use force to defend his sister from assault, and that therefore the use of force is justifiable. In other words, if you don't go to your sister's rescue, you are a cur and a coward. If you do, you cannot have any conscientious objection to fighting for your country in time of war, and you give away the whole Pacifist case.

This dilemma was a favorite weapon of the military tribunals during the last war. It will certainly reappear in the next. Meanwhile, it is being trotted out in innumerable private discussions. It is referred to again and again in the letters I receive from those who are in sympathy with my Peace Pledge. "What can I say in reply?" they ask.

Surely the answer is obvious. If I find a man trying to rape my sister, I naturally go for him. But I go for him with my fists, or, if it happens to be handy, my walking stick, or something else of that kind. I don't go for him with a gun or a bayonet. I do what I can to prevent him achieving his purpose—I may even, human nature being what it is, try to punish him by giving him a thrashing that he will remember—but I do not try to kill him.

Suppose I did try to kill him and succeeded, whatever the police of the Courts might say to me, I should feel that I was guilty of murder. Even if the killing had been unintentional, I should still have that sense of guilt, still be unable to forget that there was blood on my hands.

But this is not really a good analogy. Let us put our hypothetical case as nearly as possible on all fours with what happens in wartime. Either my sister is raped by a man who lives somewhere in the next county, or I am told that he is coming from the next county to rape her. And all my friends say to me: "You must not allow this. You must come with us into the next county and we'll kill as many of these brutes as we can."

If I thought this argument reasonable and acted upon it, would the fact that my sister had been raped, or that I thought somebody intended to rape her, help me when I stood in the dock charged with murder?

Well, it might. Judge and jury might say: "This man's mind is obviously unhinged," and send me to spend the rest of my life among the other criminal lunatics at Broadmoor, instead of handing me over to the hangman.[1]

Now, does it make any essential difference if we substitute another country for the next county, and the men I go out to kill are wearing uniform, and my friends and I put on another kind of uniform to kill them?

In practice, the only two important differences are these: That a great many more people—women and children as well as men—are killed before the slaughter stops; and that I am neither hanged nor shut up as a lunatic for helping to kill them.

But perhaps that is because a country at war is only a larger Broadmoor, and we are all criminal lunatics together, with the most dangerous and bloodthirsty among us running the show.

There is, however, rather more to be said on this subject of "if they raped your sister." The force of the argument depends upon the belief that rape is one of the normal incidents of warfare, and that invading armies consist of sex-mad savages.

Now, although war undoubtedly stimulates sexuality, and though there are isolated instances of rape in every campaign, I doubt very much whether the violation of women is as frequent as it is represented to be. In war, each side makes as much as possible of the excesses and "atrocities" of the other. There is always some material to serve as a basis, and this, with judicious exaggeration and embellishment, is presented to the world as evidence that the Boers, or the Germans, or the Russians, or, the Japanese, or whoever else may be the enemy for the time being, are devils incarnate. But if there were no such material, it would be invented, and the rape and atrocity propaganda would be issued just the same.

In time of Peace, if there is reason to doubt the accuracy of a particular item of news, a reputable paper will always try to confirm its truth before it is published. In time of war, the truth or falsehood of a news story is a matter of secondary importance; the really vital question is: Will its publication be useful, or otherwise, to the national cause?

---

1. Broadmoor, located in Berkshire, England, is a hospital for the criminally insane founded in 1863.

If They Raped Your Sister

You remember that extraordinary rumor of the early days of the war—that Russian troops were passing through Britain on their way to the Western Front? There was no official denial of the fantastic stories that were circulated—the rumor was of the serviceable variety. And when a telegram came from Rome announcing "the official news of the concentration of 250,000 Russian troops in France" and was submitted to the Press Bureau by the newspapers, the answer they received was "that there was no confirmation of the statements contained in it, but that there was no objection to them being published."[2]

There is a still more striking example—the strange story of the German corpse factory where the bodies of those who had died for Kaiser and Fatherland were boiled down to make oils and pig food. Arthur Ponsonby, in *Falsehood in War-time*, characterizes this as "one of the most revolting lies invented during the War," and says that its dissemination "throughout not only this country but the world, was encouraged and connived at by both the Government and the Press."[3]

He gives a series of extracts from *The Times* which show the story as it was presented to the world in 1917, and then a final extract, dated 1925, from an account of an after-dinner speech by a British Brigadier General in New York "in which he professed to tell the true story of the wartime report":

> According to General _____, the story began as propaganda for China. By transposing the caption from one of two photographs found on German prisoners to the other, he gave the impression that the Germans were making a dreadful use of their own dead soldiers. This photograph he sent to a Chinese newspaper in Shanghai. He told the familiar story of its later republication in England and of the discussion it created there. He told, too, how, when a question put in the House was referred to him, he answered it by saying that from what he knew of German mentality, he was prepared for anything.
>
> Later, said General _____, in order to support the story, what purported to be the diary of a German soldier was forged in his office. It was planned to have this discovered on a dead German by a war correspondent with a passion for German diaries,

---

2. Arthur Ponsonby, *Falsehood in War-Time: Containing an Assessment of Lies Circulated Throughout the Nations During the Great War* (London: George Allen and Unwin, 1928) 64. An English baronet and social activist, Ponsonby is famous for declaring "When war is declared, truth is the first casualty."

3. Ibid., 102.

but the plan was never carried out. The diary was now in the War Museum in London.[4]

Obviously, I think, descriptions of wholesale rape by enemy troops in wartime are a little suspect. There are two things which make it unlikely that anything of the sort will take place. First, the average man, whether he is soldier or civilian, prefers a willing partner to an unwilling one—and where troops come in contact with women at all, there are usually some of the latter who are prepared either to give, or to sell their bodies, even to an enemy. Second, the military authorities, while forced to tolerate certain manifestations of sexuality, try to keep it within bounds, and are not likely to condone rape, unless as part of a campaign of terrorism against a hostile population which is actively resisting an occupying army.[5]

There can, of course, be no possible excuse for thus unleashing the most brutal elements of an invading force against defenseless women. But then, as a Christian, I can acknowledge no valid excuse for war itself and against the stories of rape and atrocity in Belgium during the last war may be put those other stories of the fate of tiny detachments of Germans, cut off from their main body, who fell into the hands of an enraged peasantry. There was a connection between the two which suggests that, in spite of the militarists, non-resistance to an invader may be more effective in preserving a sister's honor than violence.

But the militarists are not really concerned with saving women from rape. What they want is to win wars, and this appeal to us to defend our sisters' chastity is just another recruiting device, so that they may get their cannon fodder more easily.

The conception which they are keeping alive—that women are the prize of the conqueror—is a relic of the ancient marriage by capture. It rests on the principle that might is right. I am not prepared to admit that principle. I am not prepared to revert to a state of society in which anyone who is strong enough, or has a big enough club, can knock my sister on the head

---

4. Ponsonby, *Falsehood in War-Time*, 108.

5. Sheppard didn't foresee the unfortunately common use of rape as a weapon of war. In the Second World War, invading Soviet troops brutalized German women throughout 1944–46 and the Japanese did the same thing to Chinese and Korean women. The numbers of victims are likely in the hundreds of thousands. In more recent wars, rape has been used as a weapon in the Congo, the Sudan, Yugoslavia, Rwanda, Bangladesh, and Sri Lanka. See Carol Rittner and John K. Roth, eds., *Rape: Weapon of War and Genocide* (St. Paul, MN: Paragon, 2012).

and drag her off to his cave. That is implicit in the idea that it is my job to defend my sister from rape.

I don't accept the idea because I am conscious of my own limitations and I don't want my sister to be at the mercy of any man who happens to be bigger or stronger than myself. And even if I accepted the militarists' view that the defeat of my country in war meant that my sister would be violated, that would merely be another good reason for doing all that I could to prevent war. I don't want my sister's chastity to depend on the accident of which of two generals is the more skillful strategist, or which commands the better weapons or the more numerous army. I don't think it would be fair to my sister.

VIII

Here Comes the Bogey Man!

I was talking the other day to a distinguished doctor. A mutual acquaintance was mentioned. "He's one of the 'Yes-But' people," was the medical man's comment.

The phrase seemed extraordinarily apt. It exactly "hit off" the person we were discussing. But I had not known, before this conversation, that the term was used by psychologists to describe a large group of people who have made a mess of their lives.

"They see the desirable goal," said the doctor, "yet they never get there. Often they don't even try to get there. They exaggerate whatever small difficulties may be in the way into insuperable obstacles. If there are no real difficulties, they create imaginary ones. They can't say 'Yes' without saying 'But' immediately afterwards, and the 'But' completely neutralizes the 'Yes.' For instance, a woman will tell you: 'Yes, I want to make my marriage a success'—then add at once, 'But my husband is impossible! And my mother-in-law won't stop interfering. And I don't like housework. I'm not really the domestic type at all!'"

The most obstinate and incurable of the "Yes-But" cases never find their way to a psychologist's consulting room. They are too busy running this and other countries, too busy preparing for the next war. They are the statesmen who say:

"Yes, we want Peace. Yes, we want Disarmament. Yes, we have pledged ourselves to outlaw war." And then they continue: "But—look at Russia—or Germany—or Japan. They don't want Peace. They don't want Disarmament.

Here Comes the Bogey Man!

They are getting ready for the next war. So we can't disarm. We must be prepared."

And in Russia, and Germany, and Japan, and all the other countries throughout the world, other statesmen are saying exactly the same thing.

Politics have never grown up. They are still in the nursery stage. And it's quite the wrong sort of nursery—the kind that is ruled by fear. "Hush, hush, hush! Here comes the bogey man!" "The bogies will get you if you don't watch out!"

The enlightened modern parent knows that this is the worst possible atmosphere in which to bring up a child. And the nursemaid who tries to frighten her charges in this way is quickly dismissed. But the politicians are more fortunate. The bigger and more fearsome the bogey man they conjure up, the bigger is their majority.

Now, fear operates in strange ways. A soldier, waiting in the trenches to go over the top, and growing more and more "jumpy" every minute, will welcome the order that sends him forward into battle. Anything seems better than the long drawn out agony of waiting. Action comes as a relief, whatever its consequences may be.

In very much the same way a nation which fears its neighbors, and believes they are preparing for war, may itself, in the end, precipitate the struggle which it dreads. Indeed, if you once make up your mind that war is inevitable, the temptation to choose your own moment for it—the moment most favorable to you and least propitious for your enemy—becomes overwhelmingly strong.

Here we have the explanation of the talk sometimes heard of "preventive war."

This is the great danger of "bogey man" politics. Sooner or later, fear leads to war. The nations which want "security" will try to obtain it at the point of the sword. "Where they make a desert they call it peace," said the Caledonian chief Galgacus of the Romans, and there are States today which seem to believe that they will never live in amity with their neighbors until they crush them so utterly that they can never again raise their heads.[1]

One thing is certain. Fear will never lack material on which to feed, and while it continues to determine the policies of nations, war will always find a plausible excuse.

Let us see, then, if we cannot exorcise these dangerous terrors. Let us have a look at the bogey men, and see what they amount to.

---

1. A Caledonian chieftain who battled the Romans in the year 83. The quote is attributed to him in chapter 30 of Tacitus' *Agricola*.

We Say NO!

First, the German menace—an ominous phrase, when we think of 1914.

Now, I don't like the present regime in Germany. I abhor the principles on which it is based, and detest the methods by which it is maintained. But Germany is only suffering, in a more acute form, from the same malady that afflicts her neighbors. Behind her hysterical bravado there is fear. The hand within the mailed glove is trembling. The bluff of the loud defiant words is only a mask of terror.

The Treaty of Versailles imposed a penal Peace on Germany. But it contained one clause which seemed to hold the promise of brighter and more tranquil days for Europe, because it suggested that the enforced disarmament of the vanquished would be followed by the voluntary disarmament of the victors.[2]

No attempt has been made to carry out the implied pledge of a general laying down of arms. And gradually, as the years passed, Germany was made to feel that France, at any rate, desired to keep her in a position of permanent subjection and inferiority. It was this which discredited those leaders of the Reich who had attempted to cooperate in European reconciliation, and brought the Nazis to power.

But until the very moment of Hitler's final victory the Peace movements of Germany numbered millions of adherents and anti-war literature, some of the most moving and passionate examples of which were the work of German authors, had perhaps a larger circulation and exercised a wider influence within the Reich than anywhere else in the world. The books have been burned, but those who read them remember their message. The Pacifists have been driven underground, but they have not been converted to the Goering–von Papen gospel of force.[3]

These facts, and the Communist sympathies of large numbers of workpeople, make it very doubtful whether Germany could repeat her war effort of 1914, even if she had the soldiers and the equipment. Unless in what was clearly a war of defense, her rulers could not rely on having a united nation behind them. They must know that. So, even now, when the shadow of the storm trooper falls darkly across Europe, I doubt very much whether Hitler's Reich is planning a war of revenge. But it is by no

2. The major powers, with the exception of the U.S., committed themselves in both the Treaty and the Covenant of the League of Nations to gradual disarmament.

3. An allusion to Hermann Goering (1893–1946) who at the time Sheppard wrote his book was revamping the German Air Force in direct contravention of the Versailles Treaty, and Franz von Papen (1879–1969) a career diplomat who after the Nazis' rise to power in 1933 briefly served as Hitler's Vice Chancellor.

means certain of the pacific intentions of its neighbors. Thanks to French diplomacy, the Germans see themselves as once more "encircled" by a ring of hostile States. This is perhaps the main reason for the rearmament which has given the rest of Europe so much concern.

It may be that the Nazi glorification of war springs, in part at least, from the same cause. If a Government believes that war is probable, it is better that the young people who must provide the cannon fodder should have romantic ideas about it.

Also, of course, a regime which is based upon violence must make some parade of force internationally as well as nationally. For the sake of their prestige at home, Herr Hitler and his colleagues had either to rearm or to secure general European disarmament. But I do not believe the rearming would have been on so spectacular a scale if there had not been genuine alarm over the warlike preparations of other States. Even the announcement of German conscription followed a provocative gesture by France in extending the term of service of her conscripts.

Especially do the present rulers of Germany fear Russia. The Soviet Union commands limitless natural resources and colossal reserves of manpower. It is organized on a war basis. And there is an important minority of the Germany people who would give their allegiance far more readily to the Hammer and Sickle than to the Crooked Cross.

We may think that this German fear of Russia is absurd, or that it is merely a convenient excuse for rearmament. But not so long ago Russia was our bogey too, and there are still many British people who consider the Bolsheviks a much more real danger than Hitler's goose-stepping conscripts. And Germany is much nearer Russia than we are.

So let us examine next the Russian bogey—try to find out whether the Soviets are really a menace to Germany, or to ourselves, or to anyone else.

The Red Army is certainly large. It is probably better equipped than the old Tsarist army ever was. It has the backing of a far more comprehensive industrial organization. The Red Air Force is said to be the biggest in the world. And the story of the *Chelyuskin* rescues suggests that its flying men lack neither courage nor skill.[4] Communism, too, is an international creed, and at one time the rulers of Russia believed that they must bring about world revolution or perish.

4. The SS *Chelyuskin* was a Soviet steamship trapped and crushed by ice in 1934 while traveling the Northern Maritime Route between Murmansk and Vladivostok. The crew members managed to rig a landing strip on the ice after the ship sank, and were eventually rescued by Soviet airplane pilots who skillfully and courageously navigated onto the ice.

We Say NO!

To that extent Germany's fears, and the fears of so many people in other lands, might seem to be justified. But why has Russia organized for war? Primarily because she feared a concerted attack upon her by the Powers. And, in view of the backing which we gave to Denikin and Koltchak in their efforts to overthrow the Bolshevik Government, this particular bogey was not altogether without substance.[5]

We must also remember that the most sweeping and complete scheme of disarmament ever put before the League of Nations was proposed by Russia.[6] Unless we accept the view that it was only brought forward to be rejected, that fact suggests that Russian armaments are genuinely defensive in character.

The Soviet Government probably realizes now that there is no longer any danger of a League of the Capitalist Powers invading Russia. But it has been alarmed by the claims of Germany to be the champion of European civilization against Communism, and is also afraid of Japanese aggression in the East.

I do not believe, however, that Russia wants war, either with Germany or Japan. Her vast experiments in politics and economics depend for their success on the maintenance of Peace. And she appears to have abandoned, at least for the time being, her former dreams of a world rising of the proletariat.

There is another consideration that must always be in the minds of the Communists. The Russian Revolution was only made possible by war—it was the passionate desire for Peace of the workers and peasants, and the soldiers, that gave Lenin his opportunity. What one war brought into being, another may destroy.

Trotsky was sufficiently of the Napoleonic type to have taken the risk. Were he in control of Russia's destinies today, the situation in Europe and the Far East would be far more dangerous. But he is in exile, and his supplanters have neither his abilities nor his ambition.

Japan is, at least superficially, a different proposition. Towards China, towards Russia, towards the United States, towards the League of Nations,

5. Anton Denikin (1872–1947) and Alexander Koltchak (1874–1920) were leaders of the anti-Bolshevik White Army during the Russian Civil War. Koltchak was captured and executed by the Bolsheviks while Denikin escaped Russia and eventually settled in the United States.

6. The Soviet proposal for complete disarmament was made and rejected on 15 March 1928 at the fifth session of the Preparatory Commission for the League of Nations Disarmament Conference.

Here Comes the Bogey Man!

her attitude has been aggressive and intransigent. She is building a new Empire on the Asiatic mainland in defiance of world opinion and the rights of other nations. She appears bent upon securing naval preponderance in the Pacific. And year by year her population grows larger, her industrial strength increases.

Russia believes that Japan means war, and her fears seem well grounded. The elaborate road and railway system now under construction in Manchukuo can have little value in Peace for many years to come, but would be of immense importance in war.[7]

Australia, also, uneasily conscious of her empty lands, yet clinging obstinately to the concept of a white man's continent, looks with suspicion and distrust upon the growing power of Japan. The Dutch see in the Japanese policy of naval expansion a threat to their possessions in the Pacific. American foreign policy is increasingly influenced by the possibility of a clash with Japan. That picturesque pre-war phrase, "the yellow peril," has taken on a formidable substance.

To some extent, however, the foreign policy of Japan, like the foreign policy of Germany, is for home consumption. The Government, faced with internal crisis, has had to pursue a "strong" policy abroad in order to maintain its position. And behind the most provocative of its actions we find the same powerful emotion that is poisoning international relations in Europe—fear.

This is the view of that able observer, Mr. Peter Fleming.[8] While believing that Russia will not be the aggressor in a new Russo-Japanese war, he says, in an article in *The Times* of March 5, 1935, that if Japan fights, "she will fight for security—a security which she cannot enjoy so long as the powerful bombers of the Ussuri airfields are within a few hours' flight of Tokyo and Osaka."[9]

There is evidence, too, that Japan regards the former German islands in the Pacific, which were placed under her mandate by the League of Nations in 1919, as principally important for their value in defense.[10] It is true that, by her control of these islands, Japan, in the words of Captain D. H. Cole,

---

7. Also known as Manchuria, Manchukuo was seized by Japan in 1931. A puppet state was formed to serve as a launching pad for an invasion of China.

8. Peter Fleming (1907–1971) journalist and travel author who was brother to Ian Fleming, creator of the fictional spy James Bond.

9. The Ussuri River forms a portion of the Sino-Russian border.

10. The "former German islands" were Micronesia.

has "moved not merely 2,000 miles eastwards towards the United States, but 2,000 miles southwards towards Australia."[11] But there is no real cause for alarm in that fact. At the point nearest North America, these outposts of Imperial Japan are still much farther from San Francisco than New York is from Liverpool, and their distance from North Australia, although shorter, is still considerable. As Admiral Suyetsugu, until recently commander-in-chief of the Japanese combined fleet wrote, "A peculiar feature is that Japan's possession of the isles does not menace any Power, the isles being too far away from other countries. Supposing, however, that they should come into the possession of a foreign Power, or be occupied by an enemy nation, they would at once endanger Japan's defense."[12]

Japan, like the other nations of the world, is seeking security. And if she is seeking it through force and armaments, I do not know that we in the West can blame her. She is only following the example we have set.

But, on February 18, 1928, the sound of children's voices came over the ether. Some thousands of children were calling to the boys and girls of other lands, telling them that they wanted to get to know them better, that they loved them and desired to live in friendship with them.

The initiative of this moving goodwill message came from the children themselves. And they were Japanese children. Whenever I hear people talking of the yellow peril, I think of these clear young voices.[13]

We have been looking at the three principal bogies of today—Germany, Russia, Japan. What have we discovered? Not that there is less danger of wars than we imagined, because fear is all too often the prelude to violence. Any moment may produce the spark that ignites the powder magazine.

But does that mean we must sit down with folded arms and wait for war to come? Doesn't it rather suggest a way in which war may be prevented? If it is fear that is behind the increase of armaments, the growing international tension, it seems to me that the hope of Peace becomes at once immeasurably stronger. For fear can be removed.

---

11. Cole was a British veteran of World War I and prolific author on international relations and military preparedness.

12. Nobumasa Suyetsugu (1880–1944) a naval leader noted for his belligerent, undiplomatic public statements.

13. I'm unable to discover what Sheppard is referring to here. In 1927, a "Friendship Doll" exchange between children in Japan and the United States took place in the hope of promoting good will between the nations. Perhaps the 1928 broadcast had something to do with that effort.

Naturally, the process has to begin somewhere. Naturally, also, if everybody waits for someone else to take the first step, it will never begin at all. Very well, let it begin with us.

And remember, Governments are very rarely in advance of public opinion. As a rule, they lag behind it. So we must organize the will to Peace irrespective of what the official British policy, as expressed at Westminster, or Whitehall, or Geneva, or on peripatetic tours of Europe, may be. Let us tell the world that the people of Britain want Peace, that the people of Britain are not frightened of bogies, that they refuse to be scared or stampeded into war.

If enough of us say that, the Government will be compelled to amend its policy accordingly. And other peoples throughout the world will take notice. Other Governments will take notice.

Fear is infectious. Hate is infectious. We have only to look round the nations to realize that. Yes, but courage is infectious, too. And so is good will. Let us give them a chance and see what happens to the bogey men!

All very well, you say, and the sort of thing a parson is supposed to write so long as we aren't actually at war. But it is a sentimental view, and you are practical people and Governments are composed of practical people, too. I admit that the nations are arming, that war may come—in these circumstances, what can practical people do but prepare to defend themselves?

I believe that is just the one thing that is not practical. In the last war, in spite of the failure of the Belgian forts to stop the German advance, it was soon discovered that it was much easier to defend than to attack.[14] As the technique of trench warfare developed, indeed, it was shown that the cost of gaining a position was, as a rule, out of all proportion to its military value, and that a relatively weak force, if strongly entrenched, could hold its own against what seemed an overwhelming numerical superiority.

Today, that is no longer true. The efficiency and importance of the air arm have increased enormously, and there is no real defense against aircraft. So the advantage in warfare has shifted to the attack. This is an important factor in the fear complex of the nations. It is also a source of the gravest danger, because it intensifies the risk of some sudden act of aggression, undertaken under the whip of terror.

Such an attack could always be justified—at any rate to the subjects of the State which made it—if the enemy country were also organized for war.

---

14. Protective fortresses were built at the end of the nineteenth century to protect the Belgian cities of Liege, Namur, and Huy. Each was heavily fortified, and each quickly fell to the advancing German army in the first days of World War I.

It would be said—and believed—that the blow only anticipated a similar stroke which had been planned by the other nation.

But no such excuse could be advanced if the victim of the attack were unarmed. It would then stand out, without the possibility of denial or equivocation, as a wanton and unprovoked act of aggression. And men today are no longer content merely to be victorious in war. They like also to believe that they are fighting in a just cause.

So, even from the practical point of view, there is a great deal to be said in favor of disarmament. Having regard to the nature of modern warfare, and the temper of the modern world, I believe that it is the best defense. I might go farther, and say that it is the only defense.

I commend this thought to the practical people, and to the practical Governments. They tell us that there is no defense against aircraft. Here is one they have never tried.

IX

The Devil's Dividends

THE OTHER EVENING I was re-reading Shaw's *Major Barbara*, and I came to the speech in which Andrew Undershaft describes "the true faith of an Armorer":

> To give arms to all men who offer an honest price for them, without respect of persons or principles: to aristocrat and republican, to Nihilist and Tsar, to Capitalist and Socialist, to Protestant and Catholic, to burglar and policeman, to black man, white man and yellow man, to all sorts and conditions, all nationalities, all faiths, all follies, all causes and all crimes. The first Undershaft wrote up in his shop IF GOD GAVE THE HAND, LET NOT MAN WITHHOLD THE SWORD. The second wrote up ALL HAVE THE RIGHT TO FIGHT: NONE HAVE THE RIGHT TO JUDGE. The third wrote up TO MAN THE WEAPON: TO HEAVEN THE VICTORY. The fourth had no literary turn; so he did not write up anything; but he sold cannons to Napoleon under the nose of George the Third. The fifth wrote up PEACE SHALL NOT PREVAIL SAVE WITH A SWORD IN HER HAND. The sixth, my master, was the best of all. He wrote up NOTHING IS EVER DONE IN THIS WORLD UNTIL MEN ARE PREPARED TO KILL ONE ANOTHER IF IT IS NOT DONE. After that, there was nothing left for the seventh to say. So he wrote up, simply, UNASHAMED.[1]

---

1. First performed in 1904, Shaw's *Major Barbara* is a scathing indictment of arms dealers. The excerpt is from act 3.

I do not know whether or not the modern makers of armaments would accept Undershaft's creed. Some of them might prefer—or pretend to prefer—Lady Britomart's "You must simply sell cannons and weapons to people whose cause is right and just, and refuse them to foreigners and criminals."[2] But, on the whole, I think that the Undershaft attitude—or a slightly modified version of it—is more popular.

That appeared in the proceedings of the Special Committee of the United States Senate on the munitions industry, according to some of the extracts which have been available over here.[3] For instance, the head of one firm, which specialized in bombs, replied to a question whether, when the Chaco dispute was developing, their agents had not endeavored to sell to both Paraguay and Bolivia: "We do not discriminate."[4]

But we will take it that nothing of the sort does, in fact, happen. We will assume that the armament industry is carried on in the most scrupulous fashion, and that it is concerned solely with meeting a demand which already exists, and not, in any sense, with creating one.

Now, I can see the arguments by which those concerned in the manufacture of munitions—whether as directors, shareholders, or workers—will justify themselves.

"If we didn't do it, somebody else would. We may as well get the orders as let them go abroad," is only the beginning. There is much more to it than that. The makers of armaments are perfectly entitled to argue that, so long as war remains a possibility, they have a duty to the nation to perform—they must see to it that the plant and the personnel required to produce arms for defense are maintained in a state of efficiency.

There is no answer to that argument, if we say that defensive war is justified. There is no answer to it if we accept obligations under international Pacts or under the Covenant of the League of Nations which may, in certain eventualities, mean war. However much we may agree to limit

---

2. *Major Barbara*, act 3.

3. More commonly known as the Nye Committee after its chair, Gerald Nye (R-North Dakota) it was charged with investigating charges of munitions profiteering in World War I. One of the committee's findings is that munitions merchants and bankers actively lobbied for United States involvement in the war. The committee met for a year and a half between 1934-36.

4. The Chaco dispute was actually a war between Bolivia and Paraguay over oil-rich territory—the Gran Chaco region—claimed by both nations. Hostilities lasted from 1932 to 1935, with Paraguay eventually acquiring rights to most of the disputed land.

armaments, while these conditions remain, some weapons of war must be made, which means that somebody has to make them.

It can, of course, be argued that the manufacture of arms should not be left to private firms, but should be in the hands of the State. This is the view taken by an increasing number of people. But, as Mr. H N. Brailsford points out in *Property or Peace?*, this is "open to a grave objection . . . the more advanced industrial States would enjoy an undesirable advantage which might readily be abused, and backward or agricultural States would obtain the small provision of arms they required only by the favor of their greater neighbors."[5]

But I cannot agree with Mr. Brailsford's remedy of a World-Federation vested with a monopoly of Power and controlling absolutely the manufacture of arms. I have already stated my objections to it in the chapter, "Trying to Take in God."

So we come back to the position that, so long as we accept the possibility of war, we must also accept the armament firms. And Andrew Undershaft's philosophy, allowing for some Shavian exaggeration, seems fairly reasonable.

Yes—so long as we shut our eyes to what modern war is likely to do to civilization; so long as we keep Christianity out of the picture. And this book is written to express the Christian point of view.

What is the Christian answer to "the true faith of an Armorer"? I think it is precisely the same as the Christian answer to the general question of war service. It is, in essence, an appeal to the teaching of Our Lord and to the conscience of the individual.

Just as I say that it is inconsistent with the spirit of Christianity to bear arms, so I say that it is inconsistent with the spirit of Christianity to manufacture arms. I have no sympathy with the man who says, "My religion will not allow me to serve in the Forces, but I am willing to do munitions work." There were some conscientious objectors in the last war who adopted this attitude. It is a perversion of the Christian imperative which reminds me of Clough's poem, "The Latest Decalogue":

> Thou shalt not kill; but need'st not strive
> Officiously to keep alive.[6]

---

5. H. N. Brailsford, *Property or Peace?* (New York: Covici, Friede, 1934) 194. Brailsford (1873–1958), a leftwing journalist, argued that wars, regardless of their patriotic rhetoric, were fought by capitalists for profit.

6. Arthur Hugh Clough's (1819–1861) "The Latest Decalogue" is an indictment

The man who is convinced of the wickedness of war and yet engages in the manufacture of arms is like the parent who gives his children sharp knives or loaded guns to play with.

What do you think the Courts would say to such a man? Would they accept the defense: "If I hadn't given them these things, somebody else would. They were quite determined to get them"?

You think the two cases aren't parallel? Well, put it in another way. Say that two people who still believe that dueling is a reasonable and legitimate way of settling a quarrel ask you to provide them with weapons so that they can fight each other, would you do it?

If you believe that war is wrong, you aren't entitled to do anything that will help other people to engage in it. If you believe that war is of the Devil, and you hold shares in an armament firm, then the dividends which you draw are the Devil's dividends. And if you are employed in a munitions factory, then the wages which you draw are the Devil's wages.

Of course, it is easy for me to say this. But what of the man who, perhaps, has no other skill, or who knows that it is going to be exceedingly difficult to find another job, and who may have a wife and children dependent upon him?

Frankly, I can't presume to judge him. I don't know what I would do myself if I were in his place.

The case of the armament worker is different in one vital particular to that of the other people to whom my Peace Movement appeals. Those who sign its pledge are not called upon to make any sacrifice now. If war comes, it will cost them a good deal to stand fast to their word. Some of them, indeed, may be swept off their feet by war propaganda and the mass hysteria it engenders. But the very obloquy they will meet, the very magnitude of their ordeal, will help to serve the others—who will, I hope, be the vast majority—to endure all things rather than break their bond. They will feel that they are testifying to the faith that is in them, that they are standard-bearers of the Prince of Peace.

The armament worker who is asked by the logic of my argument to give up his job does have to make an immediate sacrifice. And it has no value whatever as a testimony, as a confession of faith. Nobody will bother about his reasons for stopping work except the court of referees which disallows his claim for unemployment benefit, and the wife who finds herself

---

against what he sees as the middle class' worship of wealth. "God's image nowhere shalt thou see / Save haply in the currency."

The Devil's Dividends

with no money to pay the rent or buy food for the children. His place will be filled at once, and within a week or a day his former workmates will have forgotten him.

I don't say that considerations of this sort should deter a true Christian from doing what he believes to be his duty. But even to a true Christian the inevitable suffering of his wife and youngsters here and now might seem a good deal more important than the possibility that, later on, the things he is helping to make might cause the death or mutilation of people he has never met or even heard of. And he knows that the armaments will be made anyway.

Some time ago a journalist talked to me about what he called "news value." "If a man is shot by a gunman in a London street," he said, "that is front page news. But ten thousand killed by famine in China are only worth a paragraph in a column of 'potted' foreign news."

That is because imaginative insight is limited. We must be able to visualize a thing in a familiar setting, and in some relation to ourselves, before it becomes real to us. Now the man who enlists in wartime probably has just enough imagination to realize vaguely what killing another human being may mean. But I doubt whether the man who helps to manufacture an aeroplane bomb has any clear mental picture of the ultimate destination of that bomb or the havoc it may cause. His imagination, however, can show him, vividly enough, his own home if there were no weekly pay envelope.

There is another point to consider. The armament workers aren't the only people who, believing that killing is contrary to Christianity, may yet depend for the prosperity of their homes upon war or warlike preparations. "During the past three years," wrote Mr. Peter Fleming in the article I quoted in my last chapter, "war preparations have become, after textiles, Japan's biggest industry. Apart from armament and shipbuilding firms, the number of concerns partly if not wholly dependent on Government orders for military and naval supplies of every description is immense. An Administration which stopped preparing on a big scale for war would precipitate an economic crisis."

What is true of Japan is true, in varying degree, of the other Great Powers. The stimulating effects of warlike preparations are felt in many industries not directly concerned with the manufacture of guns or armor-plate or shells or aeroplanes. It is safe to say that there are many other businesses whose profits would be substantially lower, or who might even be working at a loss, if it were not for the needs of the fighting services.

These firms may be doing, on the whole, useful work. They may even be doing essential work. But in so far as they are engaged in war preparations the man employed on armaments is entitled to ask: "What is the difference between these jobs and mine?"

Frankly, I don't suppose that many of those now working on munitions will feel impelled to give up their jobs for conscience' sake. They may tell themselves that the guns and shells they are making will probably never be used in war. I am afraid that they may be wrong, but I realize their difficulties. I have tried to describe them. And I do want to put this on record.

Some time ago I addressed a large gathering of men who derived their livelihood mainly from war preparations. I spoke to them about my Peace Movement. I made it quite clear that I was out to destroy the thing which, after all, gave them their bread and butter. They not only listened to me patiently, but many of them seemed to agree with me.

Vested interests in war are a dangerous factor, but I'm not sure that they're quite so formidable as we sometimes think. These men to whom I talked didn't want war, though it would have meant more work and more money. And when they vote at elections, I don't think that they are influenced by the thought that one party may spend more on armaments than another. They are moved by quite different considerations.

True, they won't give up their jobs while nothing else offers and there are other men waiting to go into them. Also, if in the future a Government decides to disarm, and does nothing to provide alternative employment, they will be restive and resentful. But a Ministry which had the sense and the courage to turn its back on war would, I think, almost certainly have vision and enterprise enough to provide for those who were hit by the change of policy and had no resources to fall back on. After all, war expenditure is waste, and cutting it out would release large resources for other and worthier objects.

But it is necessary, I think, for the Pacifist to realize that these vested interests in war exist, to think out the problem of alternative employment, and to be ready with an answer to the man who asks: "But what about my job?"

There may be people who, reading what I have written about the armament workers, will say: "Ah, ha! Sheppard is compromising at last! He's afraid of the logic of his own arguments."

I'm not compromising. I'm merely facing the fact that, if a man who gains his living by making armaments is convinced of the truth of my case against war, he is in a much more difficult position than his neighbor who signs the Peace Pledge but doesn't need to ask himself whether his work is consistent with its principles or not. And, frankly, I hesitate to ask any man to make sacrifices which I'm not called upon to make myself.

Remember, too, that I've worked in the East End, and that, at St. Martin-in-the-Fields, I was near not only to Whitehall and Westminster Abbey and the Houses of Parliament and the Savoy Hotel, but also to some of the worst slums in London. So I know what poverty is. I know what it does to men and women. I know what it does to little children.

Do you blame me if, in the circumstances, I prefer to look at my own responsibility rather than other people's, and ask my readers to do the same? If sufficient of us pledge ourselves never to go to war, arms may be manufactured, but they will not be used. And, as the effects of our declaration spread, even their manufacture will cease.

It is our fault, who call ourselves Christian but fail to protest against war, that armaments are still required. It is our fault that our fellow-Christians are faced with the harsh alternative: Make implements of death and destruction—or starve and watch your loved ones starve with you. If it is a sin to choose the easier way, we must share the responsibility of that sin, for it is we who have tempted our brothers, who have driven them into evil under the harsh compulsion of hunger.

Since I wrote the foregoing, I was drawn into an argument on the armament firms over a luncheon table. My neighbor solemnly assured me that there was, in this country, no vested interest of the kind I have described. And he quoted the reply of our War Office to the Disarmament Commission: "There are no firms in this country concerned mainly or largely in the manufacture of implements of war."[7]

I had not known that there was anyone who took this ingenuous statement seriously. It gained for the War Office first place for 1934 in the competition between Governments for the biggest lie of the year, the awards in which are made by an unofficial group at Geneva. But, as Professor Gilbert Murray has pointed out in a letter in *The New Statesman and Nation*, "the

---

7. Sheppard's reference is to the Conference for the Reduction and Limitation of Armaments, sponsored by member states of the League of Nations, to collect data on the production, selling, and stockpiling of military weapons and to propose strategies for their reduction. Meeting in Geneva, Switzerland during the early 1930s, the conference ceased when Hitler withdrew German participation in 1933.

prize was given only for the 'biggest' lie, not for the most skillful or plausible. It was, in fact, the old bulldog courage that won the day."[8]

But perhaps it may be taken as a sign of grace that we are lying about the armament firms. Can it be that, even in official quarters, we are a little ashamed that part of our industrial prosperity is bound up with the Devil's work?

I wonder. But it is not enough to be ashamed. We must cut out the cause of our shame.

---

8. Gilbert Murray (1866–1957) Australian-born classical scholar active in leftist political politics in England. Although not a pacifist, he was critical of arms proliferation between the wars and defended the right to conscientious objection. In *Major Barbara*, the George Bernard Shaw play Sheppard quotes at the beginning of this chapter, the character Adolphus Cusins is based on Murray.

X

The White Man's Burden

―――― ――

Do you know the story of the schoolboy who was asked who were God's chosen people, and replied "The English"? His authority was one of the Beatitudes: "Blessed are the meek: for they shall inherit the earth." "But are the English meek?" pursued the examiner.

"Why, yes sir," said the boy. "We don't swank like these foreigners. We're too busy doing things to talk about them."

It's a very old story. But the attitude of mind which it illustrates is older still. And "God's Englishman" is very far from being a joke. By a curious mixture of force and fraud, self-seeking and self-sacrifice, he has acquired an Empire upon which the sun never sets, larger in area than the dominions of any Imperial race of other days, and peopled by a more bewildering variety of nations and tribes and faiths.

He has not spared himself.

> Waves and wild wind and foreign shore
> Possess the flower of English land . . .[1]

And so God's Englishman can see no flaw in the title-deeds by which he holds nearly a quarter of the land surface of the globe. Were they not written in the blood of his ancestors?

But I am not sure that God approves so wholeheartedly of our Empire-building as the school histories suggest. And I sometimes wonder whether it was worth this prodigal spilling of human life to build jute factories on

---

1. From Oscar Wilde's bitingly anti-imperialist poem "Ave Imperatix"

the banks of the Ganges, or herd bewildered Kaffirs into the compounds of Johannesburg.

Remember, too, it is not only British blood that has been shed. When the maroons sound for the Two Minutes' Silence on Armistice Day we sometimes picture ourselves as surrounded by the great army of our fellow-countrymen who died in the war. Suppose we had a Two Minutes' Silence on Empire Day, when we thought not only of those who gave their lives that the Union Jack might be carried to the uttermost ends of the earth, but of the great multitude who perished in offering a vain resistance to our career of conquest.

They were brave men too. And they also had loved ones who mourned them.

The period of Empire-building is over. Even the most ardent of Imperialists would probably consider that we now possessed sufficient territory. But there remains the problem of guarding our gains, of how to deal with subject races aroused to a new consciousness of their subjection.

"Sleeping Asia is awakening, is stirring from one end to the other," said General Smuts in a speech delivered in February, 1935. "Two-thirds of the human race are on the move—no one knows whither."[2]

He cited "the fact that the British Parliament will this year spend most of its time in shaping a Constitution for India" as "only one indication of the situation created by the forces moving all over Asia." Then he went on to talk of Japan, her claim to naval equality with the two greatest sea Powers, Britain and America; the emergence of a Japanese "Monroe Doctrine" for Asia, and Japanese "economic penetration" in Asia and Africa.

"Even measured by the gigantic scale of events to which we have become accustomed since the Great War we are here face to face with one of the major developments in history," he declared. "By the side of this fateful situation the troubles of Europe, which now loom so large to us, are intrinsically more like petty family squabbles in comparison."

We discussed Japanese foreign policy in an earlier chapter. Here I am concerned, not with any immediate danger of war, but with that new national and racial consciousness among Eastern peoples which has so deeply impressed General Smuts. And something of the same sort, though not on the same spectacular scale, is also taking place among the African negroes.

2. Jan Christiaan Smuts (1870–1950) South African philosopher, statesman, and military leader who was instrumental in the formation of the League of Nations. Smuts' philosophy of holism, which posits that nature forms wholes greater than the sum of its parts, contributed to his vision of a confederation of nations whose interests were global rather than exclusively nationalistic.

The White Man's Burden

The awakening is, in part, a direct response to the impact on an older mode of life of Western ideas. For example, we have taught the Indians the meaning of patriotism, and the Indian nationalist movement is the result.

I remember being told by Maude Royden, who had just returned from India, of a highly significant incident.[3] She was present at a gathering where an Indian girl in her teens recited, with great fire and spirit, the first verse of Sir Cecil Spring-Rice's hymn, "The Two Fatherlands."[4] It was obvious that the country to which she vowed the service of her love was India, and that to her the stirring lines had the quality of a call to arms.

When she had finished, my friend asked why she had not recited the second verse also.

"The second verse!" repeated the girl, puzzled. "I didn't know that there was a second verse."

I am afraid that, in fact, the first verse is very much more familiar than the second, but it is to the spirit of the second that we must look if we would save humanity:

> And there's another country, I've heard of long ago;
> Most dear to them that love her, most great to them that know;
> We may not count her armies, we may not see her King;
> Her fortress is a faithful heart, her pride is suffering;
> And soul by soul and silently her shining bounds increase,
> And her ways are ways of gentleness and all her paths are peace.[5]

We have taught the people of the East many things, but we have never taught them that force is no remedy. Is it too late to teach them that? I do not know. But I do know that we can only teach them it by example. We

---

3. Maude Royden (1876–1956) British suffragist, Christian pacifist, popular preacher and author, and secretary of the Fellowship of Reconciliation. She reluctantly abandoned her pacifism when World War II broke out.

4. Cecil Spring-Rice (1959–918) British diplomat who served in the final years of his life as ambassador to the United States. He wrote his hymn "The Two Fatherlands," also often referred to as "I Vow to Thee, My Country," in 1908. The first verse is a patriotic pledge of allegiance, the second a tribute to the peaceable kingdom of heaven.

5. The first verse of Spring-Rice's hymn:
I vow to thee, my country, all earthly things above,
Entire and whole and perfect, the service of my love,
The love that asks no questions; the love that stands the test,
That lays upon the altar the dearest and the best;
The love that never falters, the love that pays the price,
The love that makes undaunted the final sacrifice.

cannot hope to lead them into the way of Christ by preaching—we must ourselves act in the spirit of Christ.

That involves a radical change in our method of dealing with subject races and of protecting British interests. And here, incidentally, is where I must part company with Mr. A. A. Milne, whose book, *Peace with Honor*, I so much admire. He would apparently still allow the use of soldiers for police purposes—for the maintenance of internal security throughout the Empire and for the protection of our fellow-countrymen outside Europe. I believe that the only course consistent with the Pacifist spirit, which is also the Christian spirit, is to renounce the use of military force altogether, and that, in the long run, this is not only Christianity but common sense.

I can imagine the derision with which this statement will be received by those "who know India (or Africa) best." I shall be told of communal riots, of Bengal terrorists, of fierce Pathan tribesmen who will swoop down on defenseless villages, of negro witch-doctors and Arab slave raiders.

But I have not forgotten these things. I agree that they must be dealt with. But I doubt very much whether we are dealing with them in the right way.

The cure for terrorism, for instance, is not repression, but freedom. "Despotism tempered by assassination" is the traditional form of government in the East. To get rid of the assassination we must discard the despotism. Terror thrives only under a tyranny, or what appears to be one.

British rule in India has conferred many benefits upon the peoples of that ancient land. But, to the Indian, it must always be an alien rule, and the Indians are becoming nation-conscious. And when political movements are suppressed and proscribed, when their leaders are imprisoned, when their newspapers are subjected to a rigorous censorship, it is not perhaps altogether surprising that there is a reversion to direct action on the part of certain impatient spirits.

Do not misunderstand me. I am not defending the terrorists. The most futile of all possible ways of criticizing a Government is by throwing bombs or firing revolvers at its representatives. But it is true that assassination is most in evidence under dictatorships and tends to disappear as other forms of political activity increase. It never survives for long in the free air of democracy.

In any case it is not necessary to have soldiers to arrest a murderer. That is a job for the police.

The White Man's Burden

I do not, you see, propose to disband the police as well as the fighting services. But I want them to be organized as are our police at home, and not on a military model.

Now the communal riots. I believe that these can be tackled as our own police tackle the fights between Catholics and Orangemen in Belfast, or Liverpool, or Glasgow. Indeed, there is evidence that they might be stopped—or prevented altogether—rather more easily. There was a case, in the beginning of 1935, where an unarmed Hindu woman, stepping fearlessly between two hostile mobs, one Mohammedan and one Hindu, succeeded in pacifying them.

We are too ready to kill to keep the peace, and it is not only Pacifists like myself who are uneasy about it. Mr. Winston Churchill has raised the question of the use of firearms in quelling rioting in India, and suggested that perhaps less drastic methods might be equally effective.

The case of the Pathan tribesmen is more difficult.[6] But here also a few good-natured, matter-of-fact policemen might work wonders. It has been noted that some of the fiercest of these bearded warriors have cheerfully allowed themselves to be separated from their guns for the purpose of taking a bus ride, and I cannot help thinking that the development of motor transport is a more hopeful method of bringing the tribes to new habits than bombing them from the air.

I know, of course, that bombing is said to be a humane measure, because warning is given in advance, and the villages are always evacuated before the planes arrive.

Assume for a moment that this is true, the fact remains that bombing destroys the results of peaceful endeavor, and to that extent tends to perpetuate wilder modes of life. A measure of security and permanence is necessary to the development of civilization.

So long as the destruction of the hill villages continues, this is denied to all who live on either side of the frontier. Tribesmen whose wealth has been destroyed from the air attempt to make good their losses by new raids, and thus bombing intensifies the very evils it is designed to end.

Even its humanity is open to grave doubt. In a letter published in the *Manchester Guardian*, May 3, 1935, Captain Philip S. Mumford, who took part in the air operations in Kurdistan in 1930–32, makes the point that,

---

6. Also known as Pashtuns, the Pathans are an ethnic group in Afghanistan and Pakistan traditionally renowned as warriors. Today, Pathans make up the majority of the Taliban.

if mild measures fail, it is almost inevitable that more drastic steps will be taken.[7] He illustrates this by describing the gradual intensification of R.A.F. action against the Kurds, and quotes from a proclamation dropped over the rebel area towards the end of the campaign:

> You, your villages, and your flocks will be attacked with machine-gun fire and bombs, some of which may not explode at once but only after some hours. You are advised to remove your women and children and all non-combatants to a place of safety, and you should not approach any place where bombs have been dropped. These operations will continue until all opposition has ceased... At the same time any others, whether they have opposed Government or not, who wish to escape inevitable misery...

In view of that threat of "inevitable misery," "whether they have opposed Government or not," the concern for the safety of non-combatants seems a little illogical. As a matter of fact, there is evidence that innocent people may be, and frequently are, the principal sufferers from punitive air action. Here is a picture of its effects by one who has seen them, Lieutenant-Colonel A. Osburn, D.S.O.,[8] as published in the *News Chronicle*, June 5, 1933:

> How many who insist that the maintenance of the British Empire depends on our aviators being allowed to bomb the flocks and herds and the women and children in Arab and Indian villages trouble to visualize what actually happens? On such occasions non-combatants are usually the chief victims. When our troops enter a bombed village the pariah dogs are already at work eating the corpses of the babies and the old women who have been killed. Many suffering from ghastly wounds, especially some of the young children, are found still alive, covered with flies and crying for water. As all uninjured adults have fled, these mutilated women and children must perforce lie unattended.

It is interesting to recall that it was the British Government's insistence on retaining this "humane" practice "for police purposes in outlying regions" that destroyed one recent attempt to secure an agreement on aerial disarmament.

7. Philip Mumford, British army officer who joined Sheppard's Peace Pledge Union and in 1937 published *An Introduction to Pacifism*. Mumford is famous for a January 1937 speech in which he asked, "What is the difference between throwing 500 babies into a fire and throwing fire from aeroplanes on 500 babies?" and answered: "None."

8. Arthur Osburn, British military officer who published *Must England Lose India?* in 1937.

The White Man's Burden

Bombing has one thing, and one thing only, to commend it—its comparative cheapness. But once the British people realizes what it entails, I believe that the Government will be forced to find some other method of civilizing native races.

This should not be impossible. There are those who believe that the tribesmen rob not because they are vicious, but because they are poor, and that if they were given a real opportunity of achieving comfort and a modest prosperity by peaceful labor the frontier raids would cease.

Is this fantastic? I shall doubtless be told so. Had I lived 250 years ago and suggested to the Master of Stair that the Highland caterans whom he hated, because they barred the way to the ordered peaceful Scotland of his dreams, could be made honest and useful citizens, he would have thought me mad. And since to him the MacIans were only a "thieving tribe," the name of Glencoe stains his name, and that of the King he served, and the page of Scottish history forever.⁹

We no longer add treachery to massacre, or pay the debt of hospitality with the sword, but there is too close a resemblance between our attitude to the hillsmen and Stair's to the Highlanders to allow me to feel altogether comfortable. And bombing a native village from the air has something of the same quality of a slaughter of the defenseless that makes our gorge rise as we read of that grim February morning in the Glen of Weeping.¹⁰

Where tribesmen kill or rob, let us punish them by all means—if we can find those who are guilty. If we cannot, we are no more entitled to adopt a policy of reprisals, which confounds innocent and guilty in a common doom, and may fall more heavily upon the innocent, than we were in Ireland when we unleashed the Black and Tans in the days of "the Troubles."¹¹

---

9. John Dalrymple (1648–1707) called the Master of Stair after the village in which he was born, was James VII's Secretary of State over Scotland in 1692 when he ordered some forty Jacobite highlanders of the MacDonald and MacIan clans massacred at Glencoe on the pretext that they were thieves.

10. A glen in the Scottish highlands, so called because it's the site of the Glencoe massacre.

11. Although 'the Troubles" is sometimes loosely used to refer to a number of periods of conflict in Northern Ireland, Sheppard means by it the Irish War of Independence (1919–1921) also sometimes called the Black and Tan War, which resulted in the creation of an Irish Free State. Black and Tans were British civilians recruited to assist Irish policemen. Their name came from their uniforms of khaki army trousers and dark police tunics and caps. The uniform was deliberately mixed to distinguish the Black and Tans from British troops on the one hand and Irish constables on the other.

The national conscience condemned that reversion to barbarism. The victims of our bombing squadrons in "outlying regions" may be farther away, but they represent just as surely a challenge to our humanity, and to that sense of justice and fair play of which we are so proud.

When we come to the witch doctors and their capacity for creating unrest among the natives of Africa, we have to ask ourselves the question: Has our treatment of these negroes been of a kind which we can conscientiously defend? In some cases, perhaps, yes. But when we think of the position, in the Union of South Africa and elsewhere, of those whose ancestors were the original owners of the soil, there is much that might make us ashamed.

I believe that, as the Africans are educated, the power of the witch doctors will wither away. I believe also that white men and black can live together amicably if the whites are prepared to show a little less suspicion and a little more goodwill. But to deny to negroes the rights of citizenship, to refuse them entry into skilled trades, to keep them permanently in a condition of semi-slavery, is to make inevitable the struggle which the European minority dreads.

We come to what is perhaps the most difficult problem of all—that of the slave raids and slave trading. These must be suppressed. But can a police force, in the ordinary sense of the term, suppress them?

I suggest that here we have a legitimate "police purpose" for which aeroplanes might be used—not to carry bombs, but to transport policemen quickly to any village which was being attacked by slave-raiders. (Aeroplanes might be used in a similar way on the Northwest Frontier of India.)[12] It is surely not beyond the wit of the administrators of native territories to devise some system by which wireless warnings of these attacks can be given, and protection be rushed by air to their victims.

Then I should deal with the slave dhows, crossing from Africa to Arabia with their tragic cargoes, not by naval ships, but by a system of police boats.

What, I may be asked, is the difference between the methods I am suggesting and those at present adopted other than a difference of name?

To my mind there is a very real distinction. A police force is, or should be, a civilian organization. Its men are subject to discipline, but not to military discipline. And the officers of the force can only act within the terms of the civil law, which they must themselves obey.

---

12. Now part of Pakistan, the Indian Northwest Frontier in the nineteenth and early twentieth centuries was the center of a lively slave trade.

But if they are to protect villages from attack by armed raiders, or to arrest slave dhows, must they not be armed, and must they not use their arms? And, if I once admit this, does not the whole case which I have built upon the basis of the Commandment, "Thou shalt not kill," come crashing to the ground?

To me that Commandment is absolute, but I think I could understand and sympathize with the man who said: "A policeman must not be sent out defenseless against armed criminals. He must not use any lethal weapon supplied to him except as a last resort, but if it is necessary to protect his own life or the lives of others, it is his duty to use it." It is possible to make out a case on those lines which would still be quite consistent with a refusal, in any circumstances, to go to war.

Remember, where you have a party of armed raiders attacking a native village for the purpose of enslaving its inhabitants, or escorting a caravan of captives, or where you have a dhow with a cargo of slaves on board, you are dealing with criminals who have been caught red-handed. In war, you are not asked to kill criminals, but people who are as decent and as law-abiding as yourself.

But I do not think that killing would be necessary. Here is a case where, I think, we could call upon science to help us. I don't pretend to know very much about the technical side of these matters, but I can see no reason why tear gas, for instance, should not be effective in demoralizing a party of slave-raiders and enabling their arrest to be effected without loss of life. It is, of course, painful and unpleasant, but it does not kill and it causes no permanent injury. It merely produces temporary disablement—and that, in the circumstances we are considering, would seem to be advisable.

So far I have dealt with these problems of the "outlying regions" in what, I hope, is a practical way. But they cannot be permanently or satisfactorily solved while the spirit of warfare and violence remains an integral part of the character of so many Eastern and African races.

I believe that, by the force of example alone, we may do much to bring these peoples to a new way of life, even if they retain their present religious beliefs. But I should also like to see a great extension of missionary activity on the part of the Christian Churches. At the moment we are increasing expenditure on preparation for war, while missionary enterprise is curtailed and restricted for lack of funds. I want to see the money now spent on armaments being diverted to uses that will benefit humanity, that will be creative and not destructive—and high among these I would place the propagation of the Gospel of Christ.

It may take centuries to win Africa and Asia to Christianity. It may never be accomplished completely. But it is well worth trying to do. Indeed, it is our duty as Christians to attempt it. And we may find it much easier to make converts if we no longer repudiate Christ in our actions while we preach Him with our lips. What is the use of telling natives about the Sermon on the Mount or the sacrifice which Our Lord made for all men if, at the same time, we deny them elementary human rights and if, behind the picture we present of the Prince of Peace, they see guns and soldiers and battleships and bombing aeroplanes?

One of the most hopeful signs of today in the mission field is, therefore, the decision of a number of missionary societies and individual missionaries that they do not desire any use or threat of force to be made in order to protect their lives or property. I believe that, even if, for the time being, that increases the dangers of their calling, it will also enhance vastly their moral authority and bring many new converts to their schools and churches.

I know what magic attaches to the word "prestige," and how we like to feel that behind every man, woman and child of our race in the farthest corners of the earth is the might of the British Navy and of British arms. But prestige is an intangible thing. In the last analysis, it depends not upon battleships and armies, but upon personality. When I hear the advocates of repression within the Empire and the diplomacy of menace outside its boundaries talk of prestige, I think of the Matabele rebellion of 1896.

There is very little in common between my point of view as a Pacifist and that of Cecil John Rhodes, who dreamed of Empire and spared neither himself nor others to make his dreams come true.[13] But Rhodes' method of dealing with that native rising was based upon a realization that there is something in the soul of man which is stronger than all the weapons of war.

Leaving behind the troops who had been called out to quell the revolt, he went unarmed into the Matabele country, and met the rebel chiefs in council among the Matoppo hills.

To my mind that was the greatest moment of Rhodes' life, and the story of this strange peace conference is worth a hundred tales of battle. But perhaps you think that the prestige of the white man would have stood

13. Cecil John Rhodes (1853–1902) British imperialist for whom Rhodesia, now Zimbabwe, was named. The Matabele Revolt occurred in July 1896. Several white settlers were slain before Rhodes managed to pacify the Matabele warriors at a meeting in the Matoppo hills.

higher if the Matabele had been defeated in the field, and British soldiers had carried fire and sword through the native kraals?

That way would have left behind it resentment and bitterness and tragic memories and the spirit of hatred and revenge. The way which Rhodes chose left the memory of a supreme act of faith and courage on the part of one man who risked his own life to prevent the death of thousands. The chiefs who faced him at that historic meeting in the Matoppos were all brave men. They were willing to accept the chances of war. But none of them would willingly have ventured, thus alone and unarmed, into the midst of his enemies, and they recognized and saluted in Rhodes a courage that was greater than their own. I should say that the prestige of Britain never stood higher in Africa than at the moment when Rhodes returned from the hills with the news that the rebellion was at an end.

The only prestige that is worth having depends upon moral qualities. The only Empire that is worth having rests upon the free consent of free peoples. I believe that this applies equally to our dealings with native races as to our relations with the white Dominions, and that the whole of British policy throughout the world should be guided and inspired by these principles.

What is the alternative? Remember General Smuts' warning "Two-thirds of the human race are on the move—no one knows whither." Unless white and brown and black and yellow can live amicably together, in twenty, fifty, or a hundred years' time we will inevitably be faced by wars of color.

Already Japan is fully equipped as a naval and military Power. Britain and France have both trained large numbers of native troops. European officers have drilled and organized colored armies in independent States both in Asia and Africa. There is thus being built up at least the nucleus of a formidable war machine which may one day be turned against the white races.

Nor could we afford to despise these antagonists. Among them are some of the finest fighting men in the world. They are nurtured in a fatalism that makes them indifferent to death. And they have the weight of numbers on their side.

In the British Empire there are seventy million whites and a colored population of over three hundred and seventy millions. And what sort of force could Europe put into the field against the hosts of Asia? Remember, too, that the disproportion tends to increase rather than diminish. With every year that passes, the fecundity of the East lengthens the odds against us.

Can we, in these circumstances, afford to rely upon war, or the instruments of war, to preserve our distinctive European culture? I am afraid that if we do, we are doomed.

Here, from the purely practical point of view, is the most tremendous of all the arguments for Pacifism. At the moment the West is in the position of world leadership. Western ideas and modes of life are being grafted upon the ancient civilizations of the East and upon the traditional simplicities of primitive peoples. If the West continues to rely upon force, to act upon the principle that it is war and conquest which exalt nations, the colored races will learn that lesson with the rest, and the day will come when our pupils will destroy us.

But if there is to be permanent peace between white men and those of other colors, we must renounce not only aggression and violence, but also the psychology which makes these things so fatally easy. We must put a period to this loose talk of superior and inferior races. We were barbarians for long centuries after the East had attained a high level of culture. We owe our religion to a primitive shepherd tribe whose original home was in the waterless wastes of the Arabian desert and who were the slaves, in turn, of Egypt, of Babylon, and of Rome. The negroes may be less developed than we are, but how much of the difference between us is due to disparity of opportunity? The mission schools today are turning out a type of educated African of which any race might be proud. And who, hearing Paul Robeson's glorious voice, or seeing him act, can hug to himself the delusion of superiority?

I remember an old Scot who, whenever the claims of long descent were urged, would remark: "Aweel, we're a' Jock Tamson's bairns."[14] Overriding all differences of race and blood there is a common brotherhood of man. We are all members of one great family. It was man, and not specifically the white man, who was made in the image of God.

---

14. A popular Scottish saying that connotes "We're all the same under the skin" or, less commonly, "we're all children of one God."

XI

Red Dawn, Black Night

"I AM OPPOSED TO all capitalist war."

How often do we hear that statement today. Those who make it go on to say that the motive, the driving force behind war is always the pressure of an economic necessity, and that, so long as capitalism exists, war will continue.

The remedy, we are told, is international Socialism. Sometimes it is suggested that this may be attained by a process of peaceful evolution. But a large and influential body of Socialist opinion, including many people who are not Communists, believe that a period of revolution and civil war must precede the transformation of the existing order.

Here we are faced with the idea of the "war to end war" in a slightly different form. But the fundamental fallacy, the fatal error, is preserved intact. It lies in the belief that, although war generally is wrong, one particular kind of war is right.

Any discussion of general Socialist or Communist doctrine is outside the scope of this book. I may say, however, that I am not unsympathetic to those who desire to spread the good things of life more evenly over the whole population. I do not believe that any society can be truly Christian in which a few individuals are enormously wealthy while the great mass of the population lives continually under the shadow of economic insecurity and large numbers of families are poised on the razor-edge that divides poverty from destitution. And there are times when I wonder if perhaps some form of Socialism may not be necessary to provide a way of escape from the paradox of want in the midst of superabundance.

But however desirable this end may be, I am not prepared to purchase it at the price of bloodshed. I do not believe that a civil war, waged in order to dispossess the capitalists, is different from any other sort of war. I do not know of any qualifying clause to the Commandment, "Thou shalt not kill," which makes the slaughter of capitalists or their supporters a meritorious act. Even if we adopt the fashionable euphemism, and call it "liquidation," it still remains murder.

I am writing, of course, from the Christian standpoint, and the Marxian Socialist rejects religion as "the opium of the people." He would find in my condemnation of proletarian war merely another proof of the statement of Marx that "the social principles of Christianity preach cowardice, self-contempt, abasement, submission, humility, in a word, all the qualities of the canaille . . . the social principles of Christianity are lick-spittle."[1]

There are, however, a number of people who seek to reconcile the teachings of Our Lord with revolutionary Socialism. I do not doubt their sincerity, but I would ask them to re-read the second, third, and fourth chapters of this book, and to apply the arguments and the quotations they find there, not to the wars of nations, but to those of classes. Or, better still, let them go to the fountainhead and re-read their New Testament, keeping the same application in mind.

But that, I may be told, gets us nowhere. "I have no intention," says the Christian revolutionary, "of starting a war. It would be both wicked and foolish to attempt anything of the kind. I visualize a situation in which the nations are again at grips, and the only way to restore peace is by means of a rising of the proletariat which will overthrow the Government. If we choose our moment correctly we will be able to repeat the coup of Lenin in Russia, and at the same time put an end to the war and establish Socialism."

This, you see, is a rather more subtle form of the "war to end war." We are to have a little killing in order to put a stop to slaughter on a much larger scale. And it is suggested that those killed will mainly be the persons who were responsible for beginning or for carrying on the foreign war.

Unfortunately, as the case of Russia shows, the revolutionary coup may only be the beginning of a long period of civil war. Fratricidal strife is just as wasteful of human life as any foreign adventure. Indeed, it is usually more merciless. Throughout the years of civil war in Russia, prisoners were taken only to be put to death, very often by torture. Both sides called terror

---

1. Marx published this often quoted outburst in 1847 in the *Deutsch Baseler Zeitung*.

to their aid, and there were wholesale massacres not only of soldiers, but also of non-combatants.

The Christian revolutionary will be powerless to prevent a repetition of these happenings. Either he must wade through blood with the most ruthless Communist of them all, or he will find himself in prison—perhaps be shot as a traitor to the cause. There are no half measures in war. Least of all can there be half measures in civil war. Every man in the two opposing forces fights with a rope around his neck. For Nelson it was "Victory or Westminster Abbey"; for the Socialist who has appealed to arms, and for the man who fights on the other side, it is "Victory or the scaffold."[2]

I want the Christian revolutionary to realize those facts now—before it is too late. I would also like, in passing, to ask the non-Socialist, who might find revolution distinctly uncomfortable, to reflect that, if we were again embroiled in a foreign war, such a situation as I have envisaged would very probably occur and that, whatever the results of my appeal to the Christian revolutionary, Communist elements would certainly take advantage of it.

Side by side with the Communist and Socialist revolutionary movement there has grown up, in our own day, the curious phenomenon which we call Fascism.

Like Socialism, Fascism is a protest. Again like Socialism, it exalts the State and abases the individual. It sets up a Dictatorship as complete as that of the Communists in Russia. But where Socialism seeks to make the working class supreme and to abolish capitalism, Fascism proclaims the nation, and subordinates all classes to what it considers the national interest.

At first sight this might appear an improvement on the concept of the class war and the dictatorship of the proletariat. In actual fact, because Socialism challenges capitalism in the name of the workers, Fascism constitutes itself as the defender of private property, and the growth of the two movements in any country sets the stage for civil war.

At the moment, neither Communism nor Fascism seriously menaces British democracy. But Fascism started in a very small way in both Italy and Germany, and the Communist Party in Russia was by no means large when it seized power in 1917.

We must also face the fact that, so long as poverty and unemployment continue, both movements are likely to grow. And, as behind the nominal

---

2. Attributed to Admiral Sir Horatio Nelson (1758–1805) before the Battle of the Nile in August 1797, in which Nelson soundly defeated Napoleon's fleet. An alternate version is "Before this time tomorrow I shall have gained a peerage or Westminster Abbey!"

membership of the Communist Party there are considerable numbers of revolutionary Socialists, or Socialists who might be won over to revolutionary tactics in favorable circumstances, so behind the Blackshirts are many young people who might, in an emergency, be persuaded that Fascism was the only way to save the country from Socialism.

There are, indeed, people who are joining the Fascists today because they believe that, in the long run, the great political struggle of the twentieth century will lie between Communism and Fascism. Democracy, one of them told me the other day, is "dead and damned." The same man advanced the argument, which I had not heard before, that Fascism was the only hope of saving the Christian religion, which the Communists were determined to root out.

As I pictured the Fascists in this new guise of champions of Christianity, I recalled the words of the Duke of Wellington as he inspected some new levies: "I don't know what they may do to the enemy, but, by God, they frighten me!"

I am not thinking now of the aberrations of the neo-Pagans in Germany, or of the attempts of certain Churchmen to produce a Teutonic Christ in a brown shirt, who clicks his heels and says "Heil, Hitler!" in the right places.[3] I have in mind rather the denial of liberty of conscience which is implicit in the concept of the authoritarian State. It is no use preserving the Churches if their religion is only to be an empty shell, with no relevance to everyday life. I want the substance of Christianity, not its shadow; a living faith and not a dead ritual. And that is impossible if Caesar is to be God's interpreter.

This, however, is the claim which Fascism makes. It regards the Church as a Department of State. Its ministers must preach not Christianity as they see it, but Christianity lopped and trimmed to the Procrustean bed of Fascist doctrine. Its moral codes must be rewritten in the light of political expediency. God must become not the Father of all mankind, but a tribal deity. In a word, religion must cease to be a lamp for men's feet, and be made one more fetter in the chains that bind them.

---

3. A reference to the German Christian movement within Protestant churches during the Nazi regime. German Christians argued that Christianity was compatible with National Socialism and that Hitler was the fulfillment of the Reformation. They denied the canonicity of the Old Testament, "de-Judified" the New Testament, and excommunicated anyone who couldn't provide satisfactory documentation of Aryan ancestry.

Thank God, even in Germany Christians have still the strength and the courage to resist this emasculation of their faith.[4] But the fact that it has been attempted should serve as a warning.

What has this to do with Pacifism? A very great deal. If there is no law higher than the will of the State, as determined by the absolute ruler, no individual citizen has a right to refuse to bear arms. There is no appeal either to conscience or to the word of God. In Germany, indeed, it is proposed to inflict the death penalty upon anyone who is guilty of peace propaganda during wartime, or when war is threatened.

Now, a democracy may make laws against Pacifists. But it cannot deny their right to hold, or to preach their characteristic views without denying the very principles by which it lives.

In practice this means that a democratically elected Government may make, or attempt to make, Pacifists do certain things which are repugnant to them. But because Pacifists have votes, it is unlikely to introduce any measure of this kind except at a time of national emergency, and any law which it places on the statute book is liable to be repealed after the next General Election.

It is impossible, therefore, permanently to suppress Pacifism in a democracy, although, on occasion, Pacifists may be made very uncomfortable, and even sent to prison or subjected to physical torture.

There is another point. Democracy, by allowing a variety of opinions, makes it difficult for children to be fashioned to a pattern. Even in the State schools, working under an examination system which encourages "cramming" and tends to create a mass mind, the individual teacher may exercise a considerable modifying influence. And there are many independent schools in which thought and initiative are fostered, while home training is frequently the most powerful single factor in the formation of character and opinion.

The authoritarian State, on the other hand, deliberately prostitutes education to the purposes of propaganda, and allows no modifying influence. The teacher must be the mouthpiece of the State, and express only authorized views. Youth organizations continue the process of molding the receptive mind of childhood during the hours of leisure. Home life is

---

4. Protestant resistance to Hitler came primarily from the Confessing Church, formed in protest over the German Christian movement's excesses. Its public opposition was codified in the 1934 Barmen Declaration of Faith, the principal author of which was Karl Barth. Many opponents of Hitler, including Dietrich Bonhoeffer, believed that the Declaration was inadequate, focusing as it did exclusively on protesting governmental interference with the Church while ignoring social injustices such as persecution of Jews.

either reduced to a minimum, or permitted only in so far as it follows the recognized model.

It is possible, therefore, for a Dictatorship not only to deal—much more ruthlessly than a democracy, based on discussion and criticism, would dare to do—with adult Pacifists, but also to ensure that there would be no Pacifism—or virtually none—in the younger generation.

There is another reason why, as a Pacifist, I am opposed both to Communism and Fascism. Not only does the growth of these movements in any land involve a threat of civil war; not only do the States which they establish deny elementary human rights to their individual citizens; but countries which have gone Fascist or Communist are a perpetual menace to peace.

The intense nationalist spirit which Fascism creates, and by which it lives, can only be kept at fever-heat if there is a definite enemy in sight. To begin with, that enemy may be at home, may consist of Communist, Socialist, Liberal or Pacifist elements in the population. Once these "undesirables" have been killed, shut up in prisons or concentration camps, or otherwise silenced, a new enemy has to be found, and is usually found in some foreign Power. This leads to diplomatic complications, to "incidents," and so, almost inevitably, in the long run to war.

It may be said, indeed, that war is the natural element of Fascism. Where you have a number of States, all putting national interests before everything else, and all equally professing a philosophy of force and violence, sooner or later there must be an appeal to the arbitrament of arms. It is impossible to conceive of a world of Fascist peoples as a peaceful world. Even if their leaders wish to avoid war, and their bellicose speeches are for internal consumption only, the emotions which they arouse so skillfully—the suspicion, the fear, the hatred—must prove too strong for them in the end. War propaganda is a boomerang that always returns.

Communism is less obviously belligerent in the international field. But no Communist State can watch with indifference the struggles of a Communist minority in a neighboring country. If ever it believes that the moment is ripe, it will intervene on their behalf.

There is one more thing I want to say. Nothing in this chapter must be taken as justifying the general strike against war which we sometimes hear discussed.

A general strike is only superficially a peaceful protest. It is a challenge to the Government of the day. Its leaders set up what is, in effect, an alternative Government. It can only be successful if it develops into revolution. I believe my own method of relying on individual pledges to have no part or lot in war to be far better.

Indeed, a general strike in a time of national emergency might easily be the signal for the setting up of a Fascist Dictatorship. The Red Dawn might be quenched in Black Night.

XII

Who Stands for Peace?

———————

It is the habit of statesmen today to lead their peoples as generals lead their armies—from behind. They no longer enunciate principles, or outline policies, which they invite men and women of like mind to support; their skill lies in ascertaining the greatest wish, the greatest fear, or the greatest prejudice of the greatest number, and building a "platform" round it.

One consequence of this is that Governments are usually less intelligent than the more intelligent sections of the electorate. Another is that, as a general rule, elections are not fought upon any issue of real importance, but upon vague and windy generalizations or picturesque catch phrases.

It is thus possible for profound changes in thought and feeling to occur within a nation, and yet find no expression in the policies of its rulers.

I believe that this is true of the attitude of the people of this country to war and war preparations and the diplomacy which is based on the threat of force. Politicians either knew nothing of foreign affairs themselves, or are convinced that the electors aren't interested in them, and that they must give the public what it wants, so they content themselves with paying lip service to peace in an occasional peroration, while they leave the experts to their job of getting ready for the next war.

There is no way of altering that, of achieving a real peace policy, unless those who are opposed to war become vocal and declare the faith that is in them. In other words, we must make a nuisance of ourselves.

It was for this reason that, in October, 1934, I addressed a letter to the Press of this country in which men who shared my views on the subject of peace and war were invited to communicate with me.[1]

"Up to now," I wrote, "the peace movement has received its main support from women, but it seems high time that men should throw their weight into the scales against war."

I expressly disclaimed any intention of forming a new organization, and I made it clear that I was acting as an individual, and not on behalf of any existing Pacifist body or of the Church. But, I said, "It seems essential to discover whether or not it be true, as we are told, that the majority of thoughtful men in this country are now convinced that war of every kind, or for any cause, is not only a denial of Christianity, but a crime against humanity, which is no longer to be permitted by civilized people."

The response to that letter was overwhelming, and very many thousands of men signed the following pledge:

"I renounce War and never again, directly or indirectly, will I support or sanction it."

Months now after the publication of the original letter in the Press postcards on which men have written and signed this pledge are coming in to the address which I had given. A few weeks ago more than 7,000 men met in London at the Albert Hall to reaffirm their pledge.[2]

Now what exactly does this pledge mean? There were certain of my correspondents who were not quite sure, and who wanted further information before they committed themselves.

"Does this rule out the R.A.M.C.[3] as well as combatant units?" was a question which recurred fairly frequently. "Am I pledging myself against all forms of war work?" was another question which many men asked. Several correspondents inquired: "If there is a blockade, and food comes to this country in ships under naval convoy, mustn't I buy it? Would that be supporting the war indirectly?"

I interpret the pledge as follows. We who have signed it have bound ourselves not to bear arms in another war. We have bound ourselves also

---

1. Sheppard's famous Peace Pledge letter, published on 16 October in the *Manchester Guardian* and other newspapers when *The London Times* refused to print it.

2. The rally, chaired by Sheppard, was held in July 1935 and was billed as "Dr. HRL Sheppard's Peace Movement." Nearly a year later, the name was changed to the Peace Pledge Union. Initially open only to men, women were admitted to the PPU starting in July 1936.

3. Royal Army Medical Corps.

not to manufacture arms or munitions of war for others to use. Moreover, we are pledged not to encourage others to do these things. If war comes again, we must bear witness against it in whatever ways may be open to us. And, in the meantime, we must do what we can to oppose policies which seem likely to lead to war.

The pledge does not mean that we refuse to succor the wounded. To do so is an elementary Christian duty. But here the doctor who is also a Pacifist finds himself in a dilemma. If he accepts a commission in the R.A.M.C. he becomes subject to military discipline, and must obey the orders of the Army medical authorities. It will be part of his duty to "patch up" men who have been through Hell and to send them back there as quickly as possible.

During the war, eighty-two percent of the wounded in the British Forces were ultimately returned to duty, sixty-four percent of them to the front line.

This was an achievement of very considerable military value. But a doctor who contributed to such a result would undoubtedly be helping to wage, and probably to prolong, the war in which he was serving as a medical officer.

But against the inhumanity of sending men back—it may be again and again—into the shambles, we must place the inhumanity of denying them the skilled aid which they require. What if all doctors, or a majority of doctors, were to say: "No, our principles will not allow us to assist the war effort of the country in this way"? Many men would die who might otherwise have been saved.

Personally, I would not like to feel that any man had lost his life because, out of a tender regard for the scruples of my own conscience, I had shut my ears to the call of human need.

There are doctors who may, perhaps, be able to aid the victims of war as civilians. There will be many wounded to care for at home in the next war. There will be disease to fight—probably disease disseminated deliberately in a mad bid for victory at any price. So the Pacifist doctor would, I think be justified in staying at home. But if the time should come when his doing so would mean that men remain unattended on the battlefield or in the field hospitals or casualty clearing stations, and the only way—or the most effective way—in which he can help them is to go to the front, then I think he must seriously reconsider his position. He is vowed to the healing of men—and to tend those who need his care is his first duty.

Who Stands for Peace?

In these circumstances, however, it would probably be easy for him to retain his civilian status. If any large number of doctors insisted on doing so, the authorities would have no option but to yield.

But I would not attempt to dissuade any man who had signed the Peace Pledge from volunteering to act as a stretcher-bearer. His doing so might release someone else for service in the firing line, and so be helping to wage the war. When I think of this question, however, I do not see it in terms of logic, but of wounded men who lie, perhaps for hours, with no one to bring them aid, or dress their wounds, or give them a drink of water or the cigarette for which they crave.

What of the chaplains? The American Churches have taken a much stronger line on this subject than those of Britain. Over 8,000 clergymen in the United States have stated, in reply to a questionnaire, that they could not conscientiously serve as official army chaplains on active service in time of war.

Now there is one obvious difficulty about this attitude. It is a refusal to take religion to those who may need it most, to those who are in the Valley of the Shadow of Death.

I do not believe that such a refusal can be justified, any more than a refusal to succor the wounded. Yet, as one American Church conference has pointed out, "a chaplain is an officer, subject to military discipline, and his loyalty is to the commands of his military superiors."

Is there a solution in the concluding part of this declaration? It goes on: "We desire to minister to the needs of soldiers and sailors, but we must serve as civilians."[4]

Impractical? The authorities would never agree? Would it still be impractical, would the authorities dare to withhold their consent if every Church in the country demanded that the present system of chaplaincy should be terminated, and be replaced by missions to the Forces for which the Churches would be responsible and which the ecclesiastical authorities would control? The answer, I think, would be the same as in the case of the doctors, to which I have already referred.

A clergyman who had signed the Peace Pledge could not, in my view, serve as a chaplain, either in war or peace; but he could accept a Church

---

4. For a fascinating account of the widespread opposition of American clergy in the 1930s to participation in war, see Gerald Lawson Sittser, *A Cautious Patriotism: The American Churches and the Second World War* (Chapel Hill: University of North Carolina Press, 1997).

appointment as a missioner to the Army, Navy or Air Force. He would then be a civilian, not an officer, and his loyalty would be to God and the Church.

One difficulty arises. Would such a clergyman, holding Pacifist views, feel it his duty to preach against war?

If the Churches had declared definitely for peace and against war, no matter on what pretext it might be waged, I do not think this would be necessary. It would be known that the Churches regarded war as contrary to Christianity. It would be known that the missioners had accepted this work not to give sanction or support to the war system, but in order to minister to souls who would otherwise be without spiritual comfort and guidance. They would not be allowed to do this if they insisted on preaching against war. Therefore, for the sake of the duty which they had undertaken, while they would say nothing which might be construed as an approval of war or an excuse for it, they would not specifically attack it.

In my view, direct Pacifist propaganda must confine itself to the civilian population. It is idle to dream that the Army, Navy or Air Force will refuse to fight in the event of war. Nor is it necessary that they should. If the will to peace is sufficiently strong in the rest of the nation, there will be no war.

If, however, Pacifists are in a minority, and war does come, and we are confronted with a new Conscription Act, or if conscription were adopted as a "precautionary" measure while we were still at peace, what would be the position of those who had signed my pledge?

In the last war, some consideration, if not a great deal, was given to those who had conscientious objections to participation in slaughter. Next time, it is unlikely that there will be any conscience clause.

Those who sign the Peace Pledge must be prepared, if they are to keep it, to face imprisonment. Some of them may be allowed to act as stretcher bearers or to do similar work, but I doubt if they will all be given this choice. And if the only alternative to the Army is prison, I hope that there will be many with sufficient strength of character to go to gaol. But it will not be easy.

Yet there is this value, if no other, in the Peace Pledge. There are many Pacifists who, even if they had never signed it, would still rather go to prison than take up arms against their fellow men. But because they have signed, and because others have signed it too, they will know that they are not alone.

I remember talking to a man who had been a conscientious objector during the war. He had been born and brought up in a little country town. He believed that war was wrong, he could not reconcile it with his

Christianity, and he held fast to this view when the hour of testing came. He saw his contemporaries, all the men of military age, march away to war. Girls whom he had known and liked in happier days "cut" him in the street or presented him with white feathers. There was no one who shared his views, no one who could even understand them. The local clergymen told him that this was a holy war. He was called "coward," "pro-German." Old friends closed their doors against him. His own family looked askance at, were ashamed of him.

Can you imagine the agony of mind that young man suffered? He went through Hell—a worse Hell than the trenches, for at least there was comradeship there. But he endured it all. And in the end he went to prison.

"I shall never forget," he told me, "the extraordinary sense of relief I experienced. I think that the day I entered the prison was the happiest day of my life. For there were other conscientious objectors there. For the first time since the beginning of the war, I realized that I was not alone."

I want to make the Peace Pledge so widely known, to obtain so many signatures to it, that, if war comes again, there will be no one who need repeat that experience, go through that agony of loneliness and isolation.

But the Peace Pledge may do much more than that. If sufficient people sign it, and act in its spirit now, we may be able to prevent war.

That must be our aim. And I believe that we should make our first objective the winning of the Churches.

They are already awakening, even if slowly, to a sense of their duty in this matter. When Dr. Reid, of Eastbourne, was elected Moderator of the General Assembly of the Presbyterian Church of England in May, 1935, he made a notable declaration:

> We are coming to see that the Church must say "No" to the methods of war and the growing militarization of all the nations. Are we to go on thinking for war and preparing for war, while fear kindles fear and armaments masquerade as symbols of security? Must the Church always be in the rear, mourning over the ruins? Is the Church following the track of humanity in its wanderings to pick up the wounded instead of leading the march?[5]

---

5. James Reid (1877–1965) Scottish clergyman who was president of the National Free Church Council of England and Wales in 1932 before becoming Moderator of the General Assembly of the Presbyterian Church of England three years later. He was the author of several books.

We Say NO!

"I see no alternative for the Churches but complete and final repudiation of war," said Dr. F. W. Norwood, of the London City Temple, when he was instituted President of the National Free Church Council in April, 1935.[6]

Similar statements by other Church leaders could be quoted. But too many of those who make them believe, as does Dr. Norwood, that the only way to prevent war is, in the last resort, to put some sort of armed force behind international law and the body which interprets it.

I am afraid that this renders their repudiation of war useless. It means that war can be justified if it is war against an aggressor. And the enemy is always the aggressor. It is our job to make the Churches realize this and induce them to abandon this last ditch of the war spirit.

It is our job also to convince all those other people who are opposed to war, but who believe that an international force, under the orders of the League of Nations, or some system of "pooled security," is the only alternative, that ours is the better way. I believe that we can do it. An encouraging feature of the Peace Ballot was the number of persons who were unwilling to support military action against an aggressor, though this was represented as a means of ensuring Peace.

Those of us who have signed the Peace Pledge should take every opportunity, at meetings of the League of Nations Union and similar bodies, in private conversation, and by means of letters to national and local newspapers, to keep the Pacifist viewpoint in the forefront of men's minds. I think that we might even copy the methods of the Peace Ballot, and try to obtain signatures to the pledge by house-to-house canvassing.

There are other ways in which we can bear testimony now to the faith that is in us. We can—and, I think, we must—refuse to lend ourselves to any preparation for war such as is involved in air raid drill for civilians or their equipment with gas masks.

There is something peculiarly devilish about this form of war preparation. It is represented as a safety measure. Those who take part in it will learn how they may safeguard themselves and their loved ones in an air attack. That is a very real inducement to compliance.

In actual fact, however, young children cannot operate an ordinary gas mask, and it is very doubtful whether any effective means of protecting them can be devised. It is doubtful even if any of the various appliances

---

6. Frederick William Norwood (1875–1958) an Australian-born Baptist, was an influential advocate of Christian pacifism who immigrated to Canada late in life. City Temple is a nonconformist church in London.

recommended can be of real service to adults. In chemical warfare offense is usually at least one jump ahead of defense. As soon as gas-proof shelters can be constructed or gas masks produced in quantity for civilians, they will be out of date. Someone will have discovered a new compound that will penetrate them.

The authorities know that. But they still want air raid drill. "Great importance is attached to the contribution which a well-informed and well-disciplined civilian population can make in hiding targets, both by day and by night."

There is also a psychological value in air raid drill from the militarist point of view. It creates the feeling that perhaps these raids won't be so bad, after all, because people can protect themselves and know what to do. It develops a habit of obedience which will be exceedingly convenient if war should come. And it is almost certain to induce resentment against the Power which is thought to be threatening us, and whose attitude makes the drill necessary.

For all these reasons I personally decline, and I hope that all who have signed the Peace Pledge will also decline, to have anything to do with these drills, whether they are voluntary or compulsory.

If we take up this attitude, does that mean we shall refuse to use gas-proof shelters or gas masks if war comes and we are caught in an air raid? To be consistent, mustn't we refuse to have anything to do with them?

The idea behind this question is the same as that of the inquiry I quoted earlier in this chapter: "If there is a blockade, and food comes to this country in ships under naval convoy, mustn't I buy it?"

The Pacifist in wartime must be prepared to endure all things rather than abandon his principles, but he is not expected to sacrifice his own life uselessly. In so far as gas-proof shelters or gas masks can provide protection, he is quite entitled to avail himself of them. Nor is there any reason why he shouldn't eat food brought to this country under convoy.

Before you condemn this as illogical I want to tell you a story.

Once upon a time there was a big house divided into flats. As usually happens in such cases, the occupants of some of these flats had grievances against their neighbors and quarrels occasionally occurred. They were "settled" in a peculiarly stupid way, by the people in one flat setting fire to the home of the neighbors whom they disliked. Usually their own rooms were badly burned before the blaze was put out, and sometimes the whole house was endangered. But that didn't stop them. This was the recognized method of conducting disputes. It had been employed as long as the oldest person in the house could remember, and before his time, ever since the house was built. And everybody said that, as long as quarrels arose—and of course there would always be quarrels—that was the only way in which they could be settled.

In spite of the losses these fires entailed, the people in the house prospered. The got more and more furniture, all of it highly inflammable. They decided that the old stone staircases and corridors were too bare, and they built wooden stairs and put parquet flooring and elaborate paneling everywhere.

After they'd done that they put barrels of petrol on every landing, because it came in handy for cleaning clothes.

Then somebody said: "But look here, this is all rather dangerous. Next time there is a row and anybody sets fire to someone else's flat, the whole house will go up with a bang and we'll all be burned alive."

So they had a meeting to talk things over. After a great deal of argument, some of them decided that the only way to make the house safe was to agree that, next time anybody set fire to a flat, they would all combine and burn his one, just to show that incendiarism didn't pay. But they couldn't get all the flats to consent to this, and everybody began to get in stocks of firelighters.

Then, when all the flats were cluttered up with firelighters, the heads of families began to say: "This is really very serious. We ought to have fire drills, so that, when the house begins to burn, we'll all know what to do and perhaps some of us will escape."

Meanwhile, in a number of the flats, one or two of the more thoughtful people had been getting restive. They said: "What's the good of fire drills? What we ought to do is to promise, and get everybody else to promise, not to start these senseless fires anymore, and to clear all these firelighters and barrels of petrol out of the house." So they refused to join in the fire drill because it wouldn't prevent the house being burned down, and would distract people's minds from the one really useful thing that could be done to make everybody safer.

And the other occupants of the flats replied: "You've no sense of duty. But remember, when the house goes up, you mustn't use our nice fire escapes. It wouldn't be consistent."

The end of the story? It hasn't an end—yet. But do you think the fire drill is really a very sensible idea, or that those who want to clear out the petrol and the firelighters, and to get a "No incendiarism" pledge from everybody, mustn't use the fire escapes if their advice is ignored and the conflagration does come?

I know it's a stupid story. It's the story of war in miniature—and there's nothing more stupid than war.

XIII

Invitation to a Circus

EVERY YEAR THOUSANDS OF people flock to see the Royal Tournament, the Aldershot Tattoo, the R.A.F. Display and similar spectacles.[1] They go, not because they like war, but because they love a show.

I believe that Peace must advertise too. I want to see a great Peace Circus touring this country, touring the whole world.

Now, the Peace circus can't be the same as other shows. It can't compete with a great military display in the matter of pageantry and color. It can't provide the sort of thrill that audiences get at Olympia during the Christmas holidays.[2] But it could, in favorable circumstances, offer to men and women everywhere something infinitely more impressive than mimic battles or daring "stunts."

Have you ever heard the crowd at a Cup Final sing "Abide with Me"?[3] Long after every detail of the match has been forgotten, that lingers in the memory.

---

1. The annual Grand Military Tournament and Assault at Arms, the largest military exhibition in the world between the world wars, was basically a series of mock battles. The Aldershot Military Tattoo, held annually in the town for which it was named, was a huge military spectacle held between 1922 and 1939. The annual Royal Air Force (R.A.F.) display included an impressive air show.

2. A horse competition, started in 1907 and held each year around Christmas at the Olympia Exhibition Center in London.

3. Since 1927, the first and last verses of the Anglican hymn "Abide with Me," written by Henry Francis Lyte (1793–1847) have been sung before each kickoff at the Football Association Final Cup.

I want to see—and hear—great gatherings of people singing the songs of Peace. I want to get them to listen to the message of Peace. I believe that they can find, in this adventure of the mind, a rich spiritual experience which they shall not forget and which may, under God, influence their lives and the lives of their children.

How can this be done? There are a number of ways—Peace marches, Peace demonstrations—which suggest themselves naturally. The Peace Circus would use these things, just as the old-fashioned circus advertised itself by a parade of the town where it was pitching its tent.

But the essence of the Peace Circus, as I see it in my dream, would be Personality.

There are certain men and women whose names are household words, who are recognized, throughout the world, as leaders in their own particular sphere of thought and activity. They are doing important things. To interrupt the work on which they are engaged means definite loss, not only to themselves, but to the whole of humanity.

But suppose a number of these men and women got together. Suppose they said to one another and to the world: "We believe that what we are doing is of permanent value to the race. But it requires a certain background—of civilization, of culture, of continuing progress. Today this background is in danger. Another world war would almost certainly destroy it and another war is all too probable. Therefore we feel that the greatest contribution we can make, our supreme duty to the race, is to abandon the work which we are doing, and to try to awaken mankind, before it is too late, to the danger in which it stands.

"We are dedicating ourselves, therefore, to the cause of Peace. We are embarking on a crusade to open men's eyes to the folly and wickedness of war. It is the only way in which we can ensure that all our effort, all our achievement in the past—and all the effort and achievement of the others who have gone before us, and whose work we continue—shall not be wasted. It is the only way in which we can ensure that we ourselves shall have successors and that, through the generations and through the centuries, the torch of knowledge shall be handed on, burning ever more brightly. We do not know how soon we will be able to return to our own work, but here, for the moment, is the one thing that we must do."

Suppose that these men and women said that. Suppose that they began a great Peace Campaign.

We Say NO!

Do you see my Peace Circus taking shape? Suppose that Albert Einstein and H. G. Wells, Henri Bergson and Bertrand Russell, and other leading scientists and philosophers came to this conclusion and went round the world preaching Peace. Suppose that they were joined by Gandhi and Tagore and Romain Rolland.[4]

Some of these outstanding personalities have already done a great deal, sacrificed a great deal, to further the cause of Peace and international understanding. But I think their power to move the world would be multiplied if they were to act together instead of separately.

These men would be "draws" in every civilized country. People would want to hear what they had to say, whether they expected to agree with it or not. Their campaign would be talked about, would make men think.

There are a number of others who might join them. Maude Royden would lend both eloquence and organizing ability to the task; Lord Ponsonby and George Lansbury are both experienced and able campaigners; A. A. Milne would add to a passionate sincerity the salt of wit. Father Coughlin, the American radio priest, whose influence stands so high throughout the United States, would find here a mission that was worthy of his crusading powers. George Lansbury would carry tremendous weight if he abandoned politics and their inevitable compromises to preach Christian Pacifism in the Peace Circus. Herbert Gray's years of endeavor in the cause of Peace would find here a fitting consummation. Siegfried Sassoon might read those poems which are so damning an indictment of war. Frank Crozier

---

4. At the invitation of the League of Nations, Einstein (1879–1955) entered into a public correspondence with Sigmund Freud in response to the question, "Is there any way of delivering humankind from the menace of war?" Their epistolary conversation was published in 1932 as *Why War?* Although H. G. Wells (1866–1946) was a backer of Britain's entry into World War I, he deplored war and wrote several utopian novels in which he imagined it a thing of the past. Henri Bergson (1859–1941) French philosopher and Nobel Laureate, published an anti-war tract in 1915, *The Meaning of the War: Life and Matter in Conflict*, in which he argued that war is a conflict between life and brute force or matter. Bertrand Russell (1872–1970) English philosopher and logician, was imprisoned for a period during World War I for his opposition to it. Mohandas Gandhi (1969–1948) is, of course, the twentieth-century's great teacher and practitioner of nonviolent resistance. His countryman, the Nobel Laureate poet and philosopher Rabindranath Tagore (1861–1941) argued in many of his poems and essays that war is an inevitable consequence of Western materialism. Romain Rolland (1866–1944) another Nobel Laureate, condemned war in his epic novel *Jean-Christophe* as well as in *Above the Battle*, a collection of essays published in 1915.

would speak with the authority of a soldier who knew, from experience, the full meaning of war.⁵

I wonder if those two redoubtable champions, George Bernard Shaw and G. K. Chesterton, would come in. There is an impish quality in G.B.S. that makes him delight in the role of Devil's Advocate, but no one can expose more convincingly the shams and follies of war. And Chesterton, if he could stop thinking in terms of the Middle Ages, would shatter the solemn conventions of militarism with gusts of Gargantuan laughter.⁶

Suppose, too, that Will Rogers could forget his hundred per cent Americanism, and give himself, for the duration of the Peace Campaign, to the world cause, that shrewd good judgment and homely wit would carry conviction to many whom more elaborate arguments left cold.

Remember, too, that Abraham Lincoln's reputation was, for a long time, that of a lawyer-politician who told funny stories.

There is another name that suggests itself to me. If only Lloyd George would do the big thing; the biggest thing he has ever done! He sees clearly the horror and the futility of war. He has no romantic illusions. If only

---

5. Maude Royden (1876–1956) suffragette, Christian pacifist, preacher, and prolific author. She deserves better remembrance than she's received. Arthur Ponsonby, 1st Baron of Shulbrede (1871–1946) World War I resister, Labor leader in the House of Lords in the 1930s, and author of *Falsehood in War-time: Propaganda Lies of the First World War* (1928) which Sheppard quotes in chapter VII. George Lansbury (1859–1940) Christian pacifist, socialist, and Labor Party leader. Like Lord Ponsonby, he was a member of Sheppard's Peace Pledge Union. A. A. Milne (1882–1956) best known for his Winnie the Pooh stories, but also the pacifist author of *Peace with Honor* (1934) which Sheppard refers to in chapters II and X. At the time Sheppard wrote *We Say NO!*, the American Roman Catholic priest Charles Coughlon (1891–1979) had founded the National Union for Social Justice, a populist movement that advocated for labor. His weekly radio broadcasts attracted an audience of millions. But Sheppard misjudged his man. After Sheppard's death, Coughlon's message became increasingly anti-Semitic and sympathetic to Hitler's and Mussolini's fascist regimes. He lost his immense influence after the attack on Pearl Harbor. Arthur Herbert Gray (1868–1956) Presbyterian minister who joined Sheppard and Maude Royden in making a public call in 1932 for a Peace Army of pacifists to travel to war zones and place themselves between contending armies. Siegfried Sassoon (1886–1967) poet and decorated World War I hero who condemned the war in both poetry and memoirs. Frank Crozier (1979–1937) brigadier general and veteran of World War I who renounced war, joined the Peace Pledge Union, and became a friend of Sheppard's. Sheppard quotes Crozier's 1930 *A Brass Hat in No Man's Land*, a brutally frank account of war, in chapter VI.

6. George Bernard Shaw (1956–1950) Irish playwright whose lifelong pacifism is reflected in plays such as "Major Barbara," which Sheppard quotes in chapter IX. G. K. Chesterton (1874–1936) although a defender of just war rather than pacifism, was, in Sheppard's estimation, a great deflater of sacred cows.

he could be convinced that there is no way, short of complete Pacifism, of exorcizing the grim specter whose wings darken the world, what an effect that would have upon the nations! In a great Peace campaign he would find the fitting crown of his amazing career. Smuts, too, who has succeeded to Balfour's place as the philosopher-statesman—would he join? He desires world Peace as much as any of us; would, I think, risk much for Peace. Could we persuade him?[7]

And what of the leaders of the Christian Churches? If a movement of this kind were launched, would they—could they—stand aside? I would like to see the Archbishop of Canterbury on the same platform as Einstein and Lloyd George and Gandhi, proclaiming the world's need for Peace, vowing himself to Peace. I should like to see all the Churches, setting aside their differences of rite and dogma and government, joining to declare their unalterable opposition to war, their allegiance to the Prince of Peace.

Because I am an Anglican, I want the Church of England to take a foremost part in this. But there is one Church whose aid is of primary importance—the Church that has a larger number of adherents and a greater influence over their lives and modes of thought than any other throughout Christendom. I refer to the Roman Catholic Church.

Before now that Church has launched Crusades. Here is an opportunity for the greatest Crusade of all—a war to end war that would indeed be worthy of the name, because it would be a war of the spirit against the sins and stupidities that create material conflict.

Imagine the effect—if the Pope put himself personally at the head of this Crusade, if "the Prisoner of the Vatican" became the Pilgrim of Peace, crossing seas and continents to declare the excommunication of war. He would win such a place in history as none who has sat in the chair of St. Peter has ever achieved before.

This would, in the eyes of many, be a bigger thing than my Peace Circus, and perhaps it is more likely to come to pass. If it did, and if the Protestant communions still held aloof hesitated, said neither "yes" nor "no," that would be the end of Protestantism.

---

7. David Lloyd George (1863–1945) Labor Party prime minister between 1916 and 1922, a strong hawk during World War I and advocate of the harshly retributive terms of the Versailles Treaty. Jan Smuts (1870–1950) South African leader and Arthur Balfour (1848–1930) Conservative Party prime minister between 1902 and 1905. Sheppard quotes Smut in chapter X.

Invitation to a Circus

But I do not believe that the other Churches would be content to leave a monopoly of Christian teaching, on the one point most vital to the modern world and to civilization as we know it, in the hands of Roman Catholics.

The Pope could not go everywhere. He would visit only the principal cities. And the same would be true of my Peace Circus. But the Pope's message would be repeated from every Roman Catholic pulpit. And I have no doubt that there would be men and women of ability and standing who would be willing to take the Peace Circus' message into every corner of the lands included in its itinerary.

But that does not exhaust the possibilities of the Peace Crusade. There remain three great fields—offering perhaps the widest opportunities of all. Wireless. The Cinema. The Press.

All three would take cognizance of the Crusade as News—and Big News. But—at least in countries like America—the Peace Circus could also buy time on the wireless and so secure for its stars greater audiences than they could get in any other way. Some of these stars, indeed, may be able to speak into a microphone but unequal to the physical strain of addressing a large meeting.

Then—why not a Peace film, or a series of Peace films? The Pope talking about Peace. Einstein, Shaw, Wells, and the others talking about Peace. Arthur Wragg drawing one of those tremendous arraignments of the bestial savagery of war that grip you by the throat. Low at work on a cartoon that strips militarism of its pretentious pomps and exposes its futility and meanness.[8]

I should like, too, to persuade Korda to make a film of the martyrdom of man upon the cross of war.[9] A picture that would show the "decisive battles" deciding exactly nothing, and all the ruin and desolation and heartbreak of the long centuries of strife.

Of if Charlie Chaplin were to help, what a film we might have of the little man, bewildered and afraid, caught up in the dreadful machinery of war.[10] I was once told—I do not know with what truth—that Chaplin's secret

---

8. Arthur Wragg (1903–1976) British illustrator and member of the Peace Pledge Union whose stark drawings often depicted anti-war themes. David Low (1891–1963) New Zealand-born illustrator whose satirical cartoons of Hitler and Mussolini in the 1930s led to the banning of his work in Germany and Italy. He was knighted shortly before his death.

9. Alexander Korda (1893–1956) Hungarian-born British film maker whose best remembered movie is probably *The Private Lives of Henry VIII*, starring Charles Laughton.

10. Chaplin never made the film Sheppard longed for, although his *Modern Times*,

ambition was to play Hamlet. Here would be a still greater role, a role that might help to change the course of history, save millions of lives!

And now the Press. Sir Harold Bellman has suggested that the advertising professions of Britain and the United States might combine to "sell" the idea of Peace.[11] I believe that, as a matter of fact, a certain amount of Peace advertisement has been carried by American papers, but there is a great deal more that might be done, if money for the purpose were available.

There are signs also of the growth among journalists of a sense that professional honor and their responsibility as individuals alike demand an especial care in dealing with, or commenting on, international affairs. We still have war scares. We still have unfair comment. We still have the distortion or the suppression of news. But journalists, as a class, are beginning to be ashamed of these things, and they are not so frequent, or so dangerous, as formerly.

Newspapers, also, depend upon the good will of the public. In so far as we create a public opinion which repudiates war and pursues Peace, we must influence the press in the same direction. And public and Press together will influence Parliament.

That is why I believe that this idea of the Peace Circus is an important one, that it holds out a new hope to Humanity.

I know, of course, that it is only a dream. But I believe that we must have the courage of our dreams. It was a dream that sent Our Lord along the road to Calvary. It was a dream that sent St. Paul out to preach to the Gentiles. A dream that changed the world.

---

released a year after *We Say NO*, depicted the life of a simple man caught up in the nightmare of modern industry. But Chaplin did release *The Great Dictator*, a biting spoof on Hitler's pretensions, three years after Sheppard's death.

11. Charles Harold Bellman (1886–1963) pioneer of the British building society movement.

XIV

Peace Need Not Be Dull

I HAVE TRIED, IN these pages, to set out, not only the Christian view of war, but also the commonsense case against this greatest and most costly of human follies. I have tried to strip it of its romantic trappings, to expose the pretenses which seek to retain it as a prerogative of the League of Nations and a guarantee of Peace.

I do not know how far I have succeeded. I cannot even be absolutely sure that I am right in all that I have written. I believe every word of it—and yet there are times when the demons of doubt assail me and ask whether perhaps, in expressing the extreme Pacifist view, I am not playing into the hands of the enemies of Peace. May there not, after all, be more practical utility, more real hope of permanent Peace, in the League of Nations and the idea of collective security? Am I in danger of injuring the cause I have at heart by putting its claims too high?

Again and again—in the silence of the night, among the manifold duties and preoccupations of the day—these questions have presented themselves, and I have tried to answer them.

I can find no final answer. I can only write down, as I have done in this book, the truth as I see it. I can only hope that, when my words are read, they will help to make people think—and perhaps to act.

But I do know this. Whatever compromise may offer the greatest chance of practical achievement now, in the long run mankind must renounce war utterly and completely, or the nations will perish in a mutual ruin. And the bold course—the extreme view—makes a far greater appeal to the heart and the imagination of mankind than the nice calculations of a colorless expediency.

I also know that Humanity will never realize its full possibilities, will never grow to its full stature, so long as war remains even a possibility.

Many pressing and urgent problems confront the world today. In every land great individual fortunes co-exist with mass poverty; wealth and unemployment, luxury and misery increase side by side and step by step. Machinery is mastering man. While, on the one hand, science increases the good things of life to a degree hitherto unheard of, on the other it clangs to the gates of promise against the hopeless hordes of destitution.

I do not believe that the paradox is inevitable, that there is no way out of the impasse in which we find ourselves. But if we are to discover a cure for poverty and its attendant evils, we must give the whole of our minds and energies to the task. We cannot afford to divert any part of our efforts to war or preparation for war.

Do you realize that when we build battleships and bombing aeroplanes we are spending money that might have bought milk for babies, or established nursery schools, or swept away slums, or helped unemployed men to make a new start on the road to independence and self-respect? Or that the thought which we give to new engines of destruction, more elaborate systems of defense, or more formidable methods of attack, might solve the riddles of expanding production and contracting markets?

The end of war would not be the end of the combative instincts. But they would be directed into new channels—"sublimated" is, I believe the fashionable word. And isn't it better that we should fight poverty and ugliness and vice and squalor and disease rather than one another?

Here, indeed, victory would be worth winning, and not an idle mockery. But victory demands an undivided effort.

Suppose that one Government—our Government—decided to show the rest of the world the way. Suppose it said: "We shall not go to war anymore, and therefore we do not require an army, or a navy, or an air force anymore. We are going to use the resources we shall thus make available to better the material condition of our people, and to finance medical and general scientific research, not only for our own benefit, but for the benefit of the world. Every discovery our scientists make will be communicated at once to all the civilized nations. We have had war loans in the past. Now we are going to have a Peace Loan. We are going to tackle the economic and social problems of today with the same wholehearted resolution that we displayed in the World War."

I think that such a declaration would have a profound effect upon the peoples of the world. And our Government—or any other Government which decided to take this step—could ensure that its decision and the reasons which had inspired it were made known throughout the earth.

State-controlled broadcasting can be used to create a chauvinistic psychology. But there is a very real sense in which wireless has obliterated the old national frontiers. While the printed word is at the mercy of censors and customs officials, the spoken word is free on the ether. It can be heard wherever there is a wireless set to receive it. And the natural instinct of the wireless enthusiast, his passion for foreign stations, provides a wide audience for any expression of ideas which is, in itself, interesting and attractive. Even if the ideas are considered objectionable, they are still listened to—and talked about. How many English Conservatives have heard the English broadcasts from Moscow and discussed them with their friends?

Wireless could be used by a Peace Government, launching an experiment of the kind we are considering, to make known its aims to the world. Even if the statements were made only in English, that language is understood by more people all over the globe than any other. But they would be translated into other tongues, and the translations broadcast. The German would be able to hear them in German, and the Frenchman in French.

And, step by step, as the great adventure proceeded, the world would be informed by wireless of the progress made.

I attach the greatest importance to broadcasting. If it is used in the right way, it can form a direct link between the nations that will make impossible the misrepresentations, the lies that lead to war. Frankness and good will can exorcise suspicion and fear, understanding replace the blind panic that sets armies on the march.

But let us visualize the realization of our dreams. Let us assume that the nations have disarmed, that the reign of universal peace has at least begun. How will Humanity fare when the bright eyes of danger no longer beckon, and the old heroic virtues are lost and forgotten?

Is heroism a monopoly of the warrior? I have known it in humble homes, where adversity has tried the souls of men and women and found them pure gold. The widowed mother, battling to give her children food and clothing and shelter and opportunity, does not see herself as a heroine, but she needs, and displays, a courage greater than the soldier's. The man who, assailed by sickness and unemployment, a prey to unmerited disaster, yet goes bravely on and tries to build up a new career from the ruins of the old, would scoff if you called him a hero. But that is what he is.

They do not face actual physical danger?

When we banish danger from the world, there will be no more life. Every time a child is born, a woman goes down into the Valley of the Shadow of Death.

For those who desire it, there will always be adventure. There are mountains to climb, seas and skies to navigate, unknown lands to explore, secrets of knowledge and healing to unveil.

Do you know the story of modern medicine—of the great discoveries that, in our own day, have solved many of the mysteries of disease and opened new avenues of cure and prevention? It is a story of brilliant intellectual effort and achievement, but it is also something infinitely more. It is a story of the most frightful risks willingly incurred, of unparalleled self-sacrifice. In this battle, Death has always retreated, but he has contested every inch of the way, and all too often the men who have given new hope and new life to others have been unable to save themselves. The milestones of medical progress are the graves of the martyrs of research.

We can never hope to make either air or ocean safe for mankind. In the future, as in the past, there will be tempest and earthquake, flood and fire, volcanic eruption and tidal wave. Wherever we are, however quietly the normal tenor of life may run, there will always be sudden emergencies to test our courage and resources; there will always be circumstances in which we shall be called upon to face the alternative of life and death—to make the decision between others and ourselves.

The greatest stories of heroism, indeed, belong to peace, not to war. Centuries hence, when all the Victoria Crosses of the Great War have been forgotten, men shall still tell how Lawrence Oates, that "very gallant gentleman," walked out into the Antarctic blizzard so that his comrades might have a chance of survival.[1]

---

1. Lawrence Oates (1880–1912) British Antarctic explorer who courageously sacrificed himself for the sake of his companions. A member of Robert Falcon Scott's ill-fated 1912 expedition to the South Pole, Oates, nearly crippled by frost-bitten feet, slowed down his four companions as they desperately tried to make their way back to their base camp. Recognizing that staying with them put their lives at risk, he deliberately walked into a blizzard. His body was never found. Despite Oates' sacrifice, his companions also perished.

Peace Need Not Be Dull

I do not think there is any reason to fear that peace will be dull. But war very often is. What the poet has called "the long littleness of life" has never been more keenly felt, or more oppressive, than in the trenches.[2]

We do not take danger or excitement out of life when we turn our backs on war—unless, indeed, we find our excitement in murder. But is life—ordinary, everyday life—any less interesting or less worthwhile because men no longer kill each other for a look or a word? Would any of us like to return to the days when every man's hand was against his neighbor's and sudden death lurked in the shadow of every thicket?

Life today is immeasurably fuller than it has ever been before. There is no longer any need to seek escape from monotony in the original blood sport, the slaughter of men.

The greater variety of interests, the vastly increased opportunities of recreation, is reflected in the decline of drunkenness. Men no longer need the artificial gaiety of intoxication. They no longer want to forget the world around them—it offers too much.

In these circumstances, the wish for war is the wish for an unhealthy and unnatural stimulation, such as the drug taker finds in heroin or hashish or cocaine. Apart from moral considerations altogether, the common sense of mankind frowns upon the dope fiend. In the same way, once our minds are cleared of inherited prejudices, we shall frown on war.

Already, indeed, except where it has been perverted by a vicious and unscrupulous propaganda, the mind of youth is overwhelmingly Pacifist. The clear eyes of the younger generation are piercing the shams of war.

In their hands lies the hope of the world. Humanity stands at the crossroads. But if youth chooses the way of comradeship and trust rather than the blind alley of fear and hatred, there is no limit which we may set to the onward march of Man. Every civilization the world has known has crashed at the end—war has overthrown it. But we, if we renounce war, have the opportunity of building a civilization which shall endure.

Nearly 100 years ago a great Jew who was also a great Englishman wrote, at the end of a book penned "in an age of political infidelity, of mean passions, and petty thoughts"—a period, in short, remarkable similar to our own:

---

2. From Frances Cornford's (1886–1960) verse about fellow poet Rupert Brooke: "A young Apollo, golden-haired, / Stands dreaming on the verge of strife, Magnificently unprepared / For the long littleness of life." Cornford was a granddaughter of Charles Darwin.

> Time, that brings all things, has brought also to the mind of England some suspicion that the idols they have so long worshipped, and the oracles that have so long deluded them, are not the true ones ... We live in an age when to be young and to be indifferent can be no longer synonymous. We must prepare for the coming hour. The claims of the Future are represented by suffering millions; and the Youth of a Nation are the Trustees of Posterity.[3]

These words are as applicable to our situation today as they were to that when the young Disraeli set them on paper. More so, perhaps, for the issues at stake are graver. If youth allows itself to be cozened or cheated or dragooned into war, there may be an end forever of all that, down the arches of the centuries, with infinite labor and sacrifice, our fathers have built; an end of all our hopes of social justice, our dreams of a fuller, richer life for all mankind.

Shall we choose Mars and the suicide of civilization, or Christ and its fulfillment? It is Youth that must decide.

3. Benjamin Disraeli, *Sybil, or The Two Nations* (London: Longmans, Green, 1913) 489.

Appendix A

Sheppard's "We Renounce War" Letter
16 October 1934

THE MAIN REASON FOR this letter, primarily addressed to men, is the fresh urgency of the present international situation, and the almost universally acknowledged lunacy of the manner in which nations are pursuing peace.

The situation is far graver than we allow ourselves to acknowledge, and the risks we are running by our present methods far graver than those which a more enlightened policy would involve.

Up to now the Peace Movement has received its main support from women, but it seems high time now that men should throw their weight into the scales against War.

I represent no Church and no peace organization of any description, but merely, I suggest, the mentality to which the average man has recently arrived without, as it seems, the knowledge of his accredited leaders in Church and State, or, for that matter, without their assistance.

It seems essential to discover whether or not it be true, as we are told, that the majority of thoughtful men in this country are now convinced that war of every kind or for any cause, is not only a denial of Christianity, but a crime against humanity, which is no longer to be permitted by civilized people.

Have we reached that state of belief?

I believe that we have, but I am certain that the time has come when we must know if that is a false or true statement.

The idea behind this letter is not to form any fresh organization, nor to call pacifists together to abuse those who conscientiously are not able to agree with them, but to attempt to discover how strong the will to peace has grown.

For myself, I believe that a vast number of male citizens who do not belong to any peace society and even dislike some of the methods of those who do, are only waiting an opportunity to declare once and for all that they have done with wars of every kind.

Many persons are avowing their determination not to use violence, not only between nations, but within the nations.

An ever-increasing dependence on excessive force is evident in the movements known as Communism and Fascism.

It is time that those men who have not hitherto acted in any public way, but who wish the repudiation of methods of violence, should come into the open.

Would those of my sex who, so far, have been silent, but are of this mind, send a postcard to me within the next fortnight, to say if they are willing to be called together in the near future to vote in support of a resolution as uncompromising as the following:

> We renounce war and never again, directly or indirectly,
> will we support or sanction another.

If the response to this letter be as large as conceivably it may be, a notice will be sent at the earliest possible moment with full particulars of the day and date on which the demonstration will be made.

Source: Sybil Morrison, *I Renounce War: The Story of the Peace Pledge Union* (London: Sheppard Press, 1962) 99–100.

Appendix B

"The Christian Attitude to War"

*A Sermon Preached by Dick Sheppard
at St. Mary Woolnoth
26 February 1937*

SPEAKING GENERALLY AND WITH considerable experience I would say that pacifism is more misunderstood and misrepresented in church circles than outside. Those who make no profession of Christianity say, rather naively, that of course if they were followers of Jesus Christ they would feel compelled to be pacifists. But the vast majority of professing Christians, and certainly an overwhelming majority of those who attend churches, do not agree.

We pacifists find ourselves about as welcome at the usual church gathering as a temperance orator at a policeman's picnic, and on that account I must express especial gratitude to the Rector here for allowing us to expound our point of view. We are also grateful to you for your willingness to hear it.

I naturally wish to state the case for Christian pacifism with respect and courtesy towards those who reject it. Verbal ferocity may be nearly as harmful to peace as physical violence, and neither you nor I have any use for the pacifist who seems to suggest that he is the only righteous and peace loving man in the world, marooned on a planet of rogues—all of whom hope soon to be blowing each other to pieces.

We all desire peace, but where I think we differ is that some people still think of war as a possible and justifiable means of settling international disputes, while others have come to regard it in its modern dress as the last word in man's futility and wickedness. These latter—among whom I am included—do not believe that a people who engage in war will be able to maintain either the old values and the ancient liberties that they desire to defend, or the new values that they desire to establish. No man who has become a man, minds dying for some noble purpose; but to die in a process which kills all human purpose—that is both futile as well as obscene. There is, incidentally, a world of difference between the old soldier's baptism of fire and a modern soldier's total immersion.

This conviction, held by an ever increasing number, that modern warfare can determine nothing, cannot save the lives, treasure and culture of those who engage in it, and that another large scale war will undoubtedly ring down the curtain on Western civilization enormously encourages, though it does not determine, the Christian attitude to war …

It is my profound conviction that the teaching of Christ, two thousand years ago, is not only the word of God for yesterday but the last word in concrete contemporary reality and commonsense for today.

Even if all the so-called wisdom of this world were ranged against the pacifist it should not make any difference whatsoever—at least so I maintain—to the attitude which the Christian must adopt. If he is asked to prepare for war there is only one answer that he can give—an uncompromising and resolute refusal.

The art of killing is the essence of war, and no Christian can uphold war unless he is prepared to kill his brother. If a man believes in the Fatherhood of God and the Brotherhood of man, war is murder and all war is civil war. The core of Christian pacifism is the belief that it is never right to take human life. It has nothing to do with quietism in the sense of immoral apathy or cowardice. Its basis is not utilitarian. It does not condemn all use of force. It is a constructive philosophy of life. It does not make an unconditional surrender to evil. It attacks with something much more effective than violence, namely the constructive power of non-violent resistance.

The man who says that Christian pacifism is a superhuman and an unnatural ideal is expressing the truth with theological exactitude, for it is a supernatural idea, and if it is to be more than the fleeting hope of a disillusioned generation it must be sought with supernatural aid. It can be pursued only in the strength of God.

For us the obligation to renounce all participation in modern warfare has a constraining power which we believe to be of God. We believe that God is always and everywhere the Father—All-mighty because All-loving.

"The Christian Attitude to War"

We believe that the way of the Cross, the way which denies that violence and the power to kill are the final arbiters in human affairs, and that the way of suffering love—*not sought but if necessary embraced*—is the only means for the redemption of the world.

We believe that modern warfare, under whatever label it is conducted, for which the only method of defense is the wholesale and indiscriminate slaughter of humanity, is not only out of date but totally and finally irreconcilable with the spirit and teaching of Jesus Christ; and that there can be no hope of Christianity prevailing or justice being established between the nations under the League of Nations or any other system whose ultimate sanction is violence. It makes very little difference if a bomb is labeled "With love from Geneva" [the headquarters of the League of Nations] or "Go to blazes" from this or that dictator.

To us pacifism is a fundamental article of our creed and the crucial issue before the Christian Church today. And to me a Church that cannot perceive that war must be anathema to Christ is apostate.

Turn to Christ's teaching. We may twist His sayings with all the perversity of ecclesiastical casuistry but we shall have a very poor case when we try to make Him bless war. The nearer we get to Calvary the more obvious, surely that truth becomes.

The Christian Church will never be destroyed by opposition, but it will indeed be in danger when its moral judgments provoke the indignation of enlightened men and compel them to believe that nothing induces us to take our Lord seriously.

May I end with a personal confession?

I am a pacifist first and last because I wish to be a sincere disciple of Jesus Christ. For me Christianity is the following of Jesus Christ in incorruptness of living; and I think we follow not merely when the going is good—by the shining lake of Galilee—but out beyond Jerusalem where the redemptive power of suffering love was perfectly and effectively consecrated for the salvation of the world.

I cannot pray to God or try to look in the face of Jesus Christ at Cana of Galilee or at Calvary and then prepare to kill my brother.

And I want to ask the leaders of the Christian Church this question:

Why—at a crisis—when a clear, reasoned and passionate lead from Christendom might arouse the world from its nightmare of terror and importance do you not give it?

Why? Surely our Master's teaching is not obscure. Why? . . .

"The Christian Attitude to War"

WHY, WHY, WHY—do you hesitate to denounce war now, today, yesterday, as the vile thing it actually is—the betrayal of God, the self-abuse of nations and a blasphemy against the future of man?

History records with dreary monotony how easily the ecclesiastical mind drifts away from the mind of Christ.

I am persuaded that the supreme test today of adherence to Christ as Lord and Master is provided by the conflict between those who say that war is inevitable and under certain unhappy circumstances justifiable, and those who when asked to prepare for it and take part in it are able to answer: Not on my life—God being my helper.

Source: Peace Pledge Union Pamphlet, 1937

www.ingramcontent.com/pod-product-compliance
Lightning Source LLC
Chambersburg PA
CBHW030858170426
43193CB00009BA/653